Praise for

THE BUSINESS OF ACTING *and*
THE NEW BUSINESS OF ACTING

"Brad Lemack is an actor's best friend. His no-nonsense approach to the business of acting provides a foundation essential for success in this industry. Brad is nurturing in his approach to setting the record straight about showbiz myths, and that's a wonderful balance. Just like his clients and students for decades, readers of Brad's books will come away feeling supported and informed... and ready to succeed!"

—Bonnie Gillespie, Cricket Feet Casting

"Where *The Business of Acting* set the foundation for a budding acting career, *The New Business of Acting* shows you how to apply that knowledge in today's evolving landscape. A wonderful resource for the beginning actor, as well as the experienced actor looking to stay ahead in Hollywood's new business model."

—Sharif Ali, Co-President, Aimee Entertainment Agency

"Read his book or get out of the business."

—Adam Ginivisian, Agent, ICM

"Much of the way I conduct myself is an attempt to match Brad's style of personal management and care he has for actors. He has always been the professional adapting and growing as the needs of the industry change. To follow him, believe in him, and absorb knowledge from him places every actor ahead of the pack. Brad teaches and shares his years of experience so that the actor can boldly succeed, rather than living in fear of Hollywood."

—Paulo Andrés, Talent Manager,
Rothman/Patino/Andrés Entertainment

D1007775

"Brad Lemack's *The New Business of Acting* goes beyond the typical advice that most books offer the aspiring and working actor. He reminds us that careers in acting should be treated like any for-profit business. His fun, practical and solid advice will inspire you to take the reigns of your career by giving it the professional detail it deserves."

Patrick Baca, CSA, Casting Director

"Brad Lemack knows this business from all sides and his ability to communicate his knowledge to others is unparalleled. In his first book, *The Business of Acting*, Brad helped thousands of actors get on track, stay focused and move forward with their careers by cutting through the confusion and hype that is so pervasive in our business. Now, thanks to his latest book, a new generation of actors is fortunate enough to have Brad's expertise to help them navigate the challenges of today's business. Always clear, warm and funny, *The New Business of Acting* is destined to become every actor's new best friend!"

—Craig Wallace, Creator, The Wallace Audition Technique, and Author, *The Best of You—Winning Auditions Your Way*

"*The Business of Acting* is a must-read for any actor." —*Back Stage*

"*The Business of Acting* will benefit every actor." —CBS Radio

"This informational book is a must for anyone who is currently a working actor or wants to become a working actor."

—*Dancer Magazine*

"Lemack…pinpoints in detail the practical considerations of being a performer. Headshots, resumes, bios, publicity—all areas of an artistic career are highlighted and illustrated, often with examples. He stresses the difference between emotional, physical

and fiscal fitness, reminding that 'a happy, healthy actor is a much better person to work with' and more apt to be successful."
—Off the Bookshelf, *Back Stage*

"This book is a must-read for anyone who hopes to have a career in Hollywood. Brad knows how to separate the art of acting from the business of acting. Understanding both is a necessity if you are to succeed. He helps you meet and conquer the challenges that you will encounter on the way to becoming a successful actor. Brad has the expertise to get your career on the right track. He has helped countless people achieve their dreams in Hollywood. His knowledge about the industry is first-rate. Thank God he is willing to share it."
—Jeremiah Comey, Acting Coach and Author,
The Art of Film Acting

"The book…is a fantastic resource for actors. I especially like the steps he gets you putting into place right now. We feel it is definitely beneficial to all emerging performers. We are sent many books, but this one is the best all-round, get-off-your-ass-and-get-to-it book."
—Dare 2 Audition, Australia

"Brad Lemack has written one of the best books on the business. Acting is a road trip. You need a plan. This book helps you do that better than any other we have read. Buy it and keep it."
—ActingOnTheWeb.com

"Brad presents the material…with great wisdom and accessibility. He is a clarifying voice with a deep and compassionate understanding of the actor's journey. He has a wealth of valuable information to share in the business and in life."
—SAG Foundation

"*The Business of Acting* seminar empowered actors to take charge and manage their careers and expectations in this industry."
—L.A. Casting, Casting Networks, Inc.

"We were enraptured with the discussion [during our Business of Acting workshop with Brad]. Learning and laughing at the same time always make the best kind of meeting. It was a tremendous success."
—Women in Film

"Rarely does a book find its way to us that offers so much to so many. *The New Business of Acting* serves as an industry bible to the novice, a source of inspiration to the battle-scarred working-and-sometimes-not-working actor, a compass for the seasoned professional and a code of ethics to all. I go here when I've lost my way, and I am reminded that my success in show business is directly proportionate to the time I devote to the business of show."
—Pamela Roylance, Actress, *Days of Our Lives* and
Little House on the Prairie

"I wish I had *The New Business of Acting* when I was first starting out. It would have helped me to understand the difference between talent and skill in the acting process—and the opportunity to understand the landscape in which I wanted to have a career would have been enormously beneficial to me. But I have it now! Brad's perspective on the casting process in this new landscape put a whole new spin on that part of the business for me. His explanation about the regulations and laws impacting how agents and managers conduct business is very important for all actors to know about. This book has helped me rethink my career strategy in a very positive, supportive and proactive way."
—Laura Bryan Birn, Actress, *The Young and the Restless*

"Finally, a comprehensive book addressing the issues we actors face in the pursuit and growth of our careers. This book analyzes the business of acting for the actor of the 21st century. Brad has developed and presents a very practical and knowledgeable approach to the complexity of life as an actor and distills his perspective in a comprehensive and supportive form without any of the usual Hollywood hype. This book is enormously helpful to those of us already in the business and it is invaluable to the actor just starting out. I have great admiration for Brad's honesty and directness, both of which are the hallmarks of this book."

—Henry Polic II, Actor, Director and Co-Star
of the television series *Webster*

"Brad's many years [in the business] gave our students insights into the business side of acting. [The book] is definitely filled with information that will benefit new and current industry professionals."

—Lillian Lehman, Department of Theatre,
California State University, Northridge

Requests to the Publisher for permission or fees should be addressed to:
Permission/Fees Department
Ingenuity Press USA
P.O. Box 69822
Los Angeles, California 90069-0822 USA

E-mail: Inquiries@IngenuityPressUSA.com

This publication is designed to provide accurate and authoritative
information in regard to the subject matter covered. It is sold with the
understanding that the publisher is not engaged in rendering career
counseling or other professional services. If expert assistance is required,
the services of a competent professional person should be sought.

Library of Congress Control Number: 2010905984
ISBN 978-0-9715410-5-4

Designed and typeset by Gopa & Ted2, Inc.
First edition: September 2010
Printed in the United States of America

Also by Brad Lemack

The Business of Acting:
Learn the Skills You Need to Build the Career You Want

the NEW BUSINESS of ACTING

HOW TO BUILD A CAREER
IN A CHANGING LANDSCAPE

BRAD LEMACK

Ingenuity Press USA

Contents

ACKNOWLEDGEMENTS

To the hundreds of students who have passed through my classes, to my family of clients, colleagues, relatives and friends, and to my husband, Mark, thank you for all you have taught me on my own journey in the business of acting and in life.

FOREWORD

WHEN I FIRST started pounding the pavement on the streets of New York looking for work as an actor, all I wanted to do was act. All my life, all I had ever wanted to do was act.

Even in elementary school, I loved being the center of attention. I was never really aware that there was a process to how the business of acting works. I just kept pounding the pavement and pursuing opportunities to act as often as I could. I thought that as an actor all you really had to do was audition, audition and audition again, which could, hopefully, lead to work, work and more work. It seemed like a simple enough concept to me.

Not until much later did I recognize that there is a big difference between an acting job and an acting career.

I spent my early years as an actor going from one acting job to another, from one play to another. But then I wanted more. I wanted that career. I wanted to be a "movie star."

Looking back on it, I am grateful for the opportunities that were given to me and for those that I generated and earned for myself. I believe that things happen when they are meant to happen, but I sometimes wonder how much sooner the career part of my acting life would have come along had I been aware that I needed to do more than just be the best actor I knew how to be.

I was busy raising a family and holding down up to three jobs to pay the bills while pursuing my acting career. Who had time to be a businessperson, as well?

I learned that acting was more than just going on an audition and getting (or not getting) a part. I learned that in order to have longevity, in order to have a career that grows, fulfills and challenges, you need to know how the business works. You need to know what expectations the business will have of you. You also need to follow your instincts and the advice of those around you whose opinions you value and whose input you trust.

I've been very blessed with a wonderful career and professional and public recognition that humbles me. I also know that you can achieve that, too. What matters is how you approach it.

Take care of business, use the skills you will learn in this book, maintain your focus and opportunity will find you. *The Business of Acting* is packed with critical information that will benefit every actor. Use it to your advantage.

I wish you success and a long-running series of your own!

Isabel Sanford

AUTHOR'S NOTE:

Isabel Sanford died in 2004 after enjoying a long and happy career in the business of acting. When I transitioned from my work as a studio/production company publicity executive into launching and heading my own talent management and public relations agency, Isabel signed on as my first client.

That was in 1982. She was starring on *The Jeffersons* at the time and the series was one of several that fell on my publicity plate at Embassy Television. We had developed a close friendship during that period and when I announced to her that I would be venturing off in the world of entrepreneurship, she eagerly offered herself up as the first client on the new roster.

What followed was more than 20 years of adventures in the business of acting that would take us both to locations and places we never imagined we would see and work opportunities that embraced the career she had achieved and recognition she had earned. In the process, we were able to build on both her popularity as a television star and her diversity as an actress.

I continue to represent Isabel today, specifically the use of her name, image and likeness, and remain honored to do so. My office is filled with memorabilia from an exceptional business partnership and warm friendship that has help to define the kind of manager and person I have become in the process.

In writing this book about the new landscape, I realized that while so many things about how we do business have, indeed, changed, the simple message contained in Isabel's foreword about working hard to create opportunity was, perhaps, more meaningful and relevant now than when she first wrote it.

The technology may have changed, the process may be different, but the necessity to look within, to embrace your passion and to follow your dream will always be rooted in the human desire for most of us to accomplish great things and to leave a legacy behind from what we have been fortunate enough to achieve.

Isabel's words about success remain alive, vital and important. I trust that you will agree.

Brad Lemack
Los Angeles, California

PREFACE

T HIS BOOK IS rooted in personal perspective and professional experience that I claim as my own. Through my many years in both the "old" business of acting and now the "new" landscape, I have had the opportunity and the exposure from which to have formed an opinion, albeit a subjective one, based on what I have seen that works, what I have experienced that has backfired and what role passion, resilience and planning plays in realizing a dream.

Admittedly, my advice to you in this book is very personal and very specific and, without a doubt, very much rooted in my philosophy that while the opportunities we seek do indeed exist, we simply need to earn them, be prepared for when they arrive, know how to recognize them and then be able to maximize them when they do appear.

This book is not intended to serve as a historical treatise on the various aspects of the business of acting covered in the chapters ahead, but, instead, to serve as a subjective, hopefully informative, overview on how the business runs that impacts and, in many cases, informs an actor's action plan for career success and the journey that will steer him or her heading in that direction.

It is my objective to provide you with an empty toolbox,

figuratively speaking, and a sort of instruction manual on how to first understand what the various tools are that should go into the box, what each is designed to do and how to effectively and strategically use them all to build the structure that will eventually be known as your career.

Of course, every assembly job first needs a plan to follow, one that is well researched and one that will throughout construction keep you on track and prevent you from putting the bathroom where the kitchen is supposed to be.

You would never build a house without a plan, nor would you set out on a journey to far-off destinations without a map to guide you. That is what this book is meant to do, to serve as your guidebook, to inform you about the sights that must be seen (and, of course, steer you away from those that should be avoided) as you create and launch your personal action plan for career success in your journey to and through the not-so-far-off land known as the new business of acting.

INTRODUCTION

W HAT IS "NEW" in the new business of acting? Only everything!

When the first printing of my first book, *The Business of Acting: Learn the Skills You Need to Build the Career You Want*, was published in 2002, the business of acting really had not changed much in years. Indeed, we had come a long way since the Hollywood studio system dissolved sometime around when television became the newest, hottest thing in entertainment. But real change in the landscape, at least for actors, was still a ways off.

In my first book, I wrote about my philosophy that talent has little, if anything at all, to do with who becomes successful as an actor. I introduced and taught non-performance skills in four basic categories that every actor needs to learn, embrace and implement in order to create and launch an empowered, strategic action plan for career success.

Those skills and those lessons still apply, even more so today. The difference between then and now is how significantly the landscape in which they need to be applied has changed.

The environment has changed so much that, while my intention, initially, was to write a second edition to the first book, it quickly became clear to me that so much had changed across the board that a new book that builds on the concepts introduced in the first book was what was needed instead.

What is also "new" in *The New Business of Acting* is my perspective. Since the publication of the first book, I have had incredible opportunities to meet, to interact with and to teach literally thousands of actors, both young, new-to-the-business and older, often previously established and "working" actors. Regardless of their age and time on their career journeys, the level of frustration and a sense of being stuck were common feelings I came across regularly.

It was not just about the issues surrounding the transition from student to wanting-to-be-working professional. I also found myself talking about the issues of survival and forward movement for artists of all ages.

I am also older and, hopefully, wiser since the publication of the first book. We are all works-in-progress and, hopefully, experience and simply living life teaches how us to be open to and adapt to changes that are better, how to evolve personally and professionally, and how to be better in and at the work we do and the person we are.

I am also smarter today than I was in 2002. I have spent over 32 more semesters in the classroom since the first book was published, both as a teacher and as a student.

It was an eye-opening and joyous challenge to return to school at age 48 in pursuit of additional education and personal growth.

Pursuing and then earning my Master of Arts degree in Theatre Arts and Dance, at California State University, Los Angeles (with a concentration in performance for social change), gave me the opportunity to be the kind of student I never was capable of being before during my undergraduate studies at Emerson College, in Boston, in the 1970s. This experience has made me a better teacher of my own classes and taught me a newfound respect for students who actually do the work.

This experience gave me a newfound appreciation for what it means to earn and give a student an "A." Having graduated from Cal State L.A. with special academic honors at the age of fifty, I respect the commitment it takes to accept the challenge of learning something new (even if or when you think you know it all). I am convinced that it is the smart student, not the most talented student, who has the greatest chance for success—and never before has this mattered in the business of acting, particularly in the new business of acting.

What does this have to do with this book? Only everything.

If you expect to quickly get all of the information and perspective you will need to create and then launch your personal action plan for career success in the first few chapters, forget it. You will have to earn that.

Any plan that stands any chance of succeeding must be rooted in an understanding, an education and a lot of knowledge about how this business works from the inside out. If you want to pass around, rather than fall into, the potholes that will inevitably turn up on your career journey, you better know everything you can about the landscape you will be traveling through.

Read through these pages. Make notes along the way. By the time you get to the action plan creation assignment, you will be fully ready and capable of creating and then launching your personal, customized, strategic and empowered action plan for your career success in the new business of acting.

CHAPTER 1

THE TRANSITION FROM STUDENT TO WORKING PROFESSIONAL

SINCE MY FIRST book was published, I have accumulated nearly ten more years experience in both the business of acting and in the academic classroom, a position that has both reinforced and reinvigorated my perspective on what it takes to successfully transition from the academic classroom to the real world for students of the performing arts.

From my vantage point, if anything has changed (and so much has), it is that the chasm between what is taught and practiced in many colleges and universities and the knowledge and perspective that is needed to create, launch and maintain a positive, forward-moving career journey has widened. The challenge, as I have experienced it, is not to ask recently graduated students to unlearn or relearn anything that they have been taught or exposed to while in college, but rather to educate themselves in how to bridge that great divide and how to apply what they have learned in an academic surrounding to the real business of acting.

I have interacted with hundreds of my own students over the

years, as well as hundreds of other teachers' students as a guest lecturer or workshop facilitator at colleges and universities all around the country. I love spending time with passionate young people; I also value the opportunity to help them begin their transitions with an understanding and hopefully, an objective look at what they have already been through in school and what that education will buy them in the real world that is the new business of acting.

It is not that acting classes, scene study classes, movement classes and related courses are not valuable. Indeed, they are. It is just that these classes are not "professional" in focus and goal; they are grade-oriented and degree-centered. This means that achieving an "A" in a performance class in college does not necessarily mean that you are ready to ace an audition—or even prepared to go on one in the first place.

But let's not jump too far ahead of ourselves. Let's first revisit *The Business of Acting* perspective on "the transition."

As a student of the performing arts, whether you have studied in school or on your own, you must, at some level, *always* be a student of the performing arts. This philosophy requires you to recognize that in order to be your best, you must always be learning something new.

When you are not working professionally, you must be engaged in other activities that are positive, helpful and reassuring to your career and to your life. Sometimes it is a class. Other times, it is the job that pays your rent until your acting career alone can support you. While I will demonstrate and discuss with you the skills that you need to build the career you want, the actual talent piece of what you bring to the world is for you alone to assess, to grow, to hone and to develop.

Great actors rarely start out that way. Have you ever seen the early films of people who you would now consider to be stars? They, like you, may have the gift of talent and for you, as it was for them, that gift requires careful nurturing and significant opportunity for it to flourish.

Your professional life assignment really is twofold: to develop your skills as a businessperson and to nurture your potential as an actor. There are only two ways to achieve this: training and experience.

When you are not working as an actor or when you are not working in a temporary other job, it is important to fill your life with activities that will benefit you as an artist. There is a wide variety of good, effective classes in Los Angeles, New York and places in between that will give you opportunities to broaden the scope of what you can do. They can help you develop new techniques and enhance what you already know. You can take lots of academic classes and read lots of books about what it is like to be a professional actor, but there is nothing that will teach you better than by getting out there with both feet and experiencing it for yourself.

Often it is the thought of beginning this experience that is the source of both the greatest invigoration and the greatest fear for the student of the performing arts who is making the transition to professional performing artist. It is like that first dive into a swimming pool or your first bungee jump (so I'm told)—exhilarating and scary at the same time.

The fear factor often plays a huge role in our hesitation to embark on anything new. Fear is rooted in lack of knowledge and preparation. Knowledge is empowerment; having all the tools you will need at your disposal is being prepared. It is impossible to drive ahead until you take the car out of park. But you also have to be sure that the tank has gas in it. Somewhat figurative, but I hope the point is well made.

As a part of the process, it is important for you to get out there and immerse yourself in the daily activities of life as a professional actor and experience how it all feels. Transitions can be difficult to make for all of us at one time or another. But as your life and the world around you keep changing, your ability to adapt will often be called upon.

From one show to another, from one set of colleagues to another, from one class to another, your life as an actor will be filled with tremendous highs and exciting challenges. If you can learn how to turn the down times into positive, constructive periods for yourself, you can avoid the "I'll never work again" blues. If you can involve yourself with projects and activities that will turn your non-acting time into opportunities for you to further develop your career and your craft, you will always look at these down times as a gift, not a scourge.

I often see in college students and in recent graduates some behavior that frustrates me. Mostly, it is the result of the environment in which they have just spent four years (or more) of their lives.

When you are in college, your goal is to get your degree. You work as hard as you can to get through classes, exams and professors who might not always be as supportive as you would hope.

Finally, graduation happens. There you are, in your cap and gown, holding the diploma you have struggled to earn and closely surrounded by school loans that most of you will soon have to begin repaying. What's next?

That diploma is very symbolic for most graduates. Most students believe that with that piece of paper in their hands, the long days and the grueling hours of study are behind them. That mindset could not be further from the truth.

The truth is that the hardest work you will ever do is still ahead of you. If a successful career as an actor is really what you want, as in any profession, you will have to work harder to achieve that success and to maintain it than you ever did to earn your diploma.

Acting students often feel ripe and ready as soon as they have finished school. They want to hit the pavement running and begin their careers right away. If this is you, this is where the road show that will become the journey of your career can first begin to get you in trouble.

It is easy to get a skewed view of the outside professional world when you are a student in any college or university class. Mostly, you know what you know because you have learned it in an academic classroom environment, from field research or from the collegiate theatre experience—and that is exactly what college is meant to provide you, all of that initial introduction and exposure, from the ground up. However, you have also been, by the nature of the experience, insulated within this community. Unfortunately, that environment is rarely an accurate reflection of life in the professional world.

You may have had the chance to audition for college or university productions. If you were a performing arts or related-major student, no doubt you were required to audition for and/or appear in many of these plays or musicals. Maybe you had the chance to audition for or play the role of the elder Aunt Eller in the school's production of *Oklahoma* or Tevye in *Fiddler on the Roof.*

Clearly, colleges and universities are presenting cutting edge, contemporary, new and experimental productions, as well as the standard Broadway classics, but the practice of casting of a 20-year-old to play a 50- or 60-year-old in any production can result in an attitude problem later on for the young actor, but it is, of course, the reality of college and university theatre.

You may have been 20 and played 50 or 60 in a school production, but that will stop after you leave college. Those experiences are at the roots of what I call actor entitlement.

Different actors display this sense of entitlement in different ways. Sometimes it is in an attitude that reads that you think you have already proven your talents through the work you have already done. Perhaps it is an attitude that reads that you think you already know everything you need to know. At other times, it is reflected in your own frustration that your career is not moving ahead as rapidly as you think it should. Maybe you think you have already paid your dues. You have not—yet.

If this is you, stop thinking and get a grip on where you are right now in your career before you cause yourself tremendous emotional trauma. The day when any of us knows everything about our professions will never come, nor should it. There is *always* something new to learn and someone new to learn from.

In order to grow, you must recognize that progress equates with growth and growth equates with learning. You would not want your doctor to stop acquiring new information and improving his skills and his technique just because he is through with medical school. You shouldn't either.

Maybe this is not you at all. But I bet you know someone to whom this applies. A sense of entitlement, if you have it, will work against you at every turn—but it may not be entirely your fault.

Schools, classes, instructors can all contribute to why you might have come away with this attitude. After all, if you have been convinced that you are a star back home, why wouldn't the professional world see you as a star, too?

In the real world, the world away from the safe haven of college and classes and community theatre, there are real 50- and 60-year-old professional actors who will audition to play the roles of 50- and 60-year-old characters.

This is not meant to demean or lessen the importance of playing these roles when you can in nonprofessional venues. However, as a young actor in the professional world, you would never get that chance. This is just one example.

You must make an honest, objective evaluation of where you fall in the mix of roles you can realistically play. How old are you, really? What is the age range you can realistically play *now*? What are some of the unique characteristics that set you apart from other actors and roles they can play? Are you of a nationality or ethnicity that makes you eligible for culturally sensitive casting? Do you speak a second or third language (other than English) well enough to qualify you to play this range of roles in professional American and non-American productions?

Your answers to these questions will ground you in what will be the truth, not the entitlement, of your career. Your answers to these questions will also help you define your brand.

Actor entitlement can get in the way of your professional growth. It can foster an attitude that will not serve you, your journey or your career well. Sorry, but you are not entitled to play whatever role you want just because you think you can play it.

You are not entitled to access and opportunity simply because you have a college degree and think it is owed to you. It is not.

Actor entitlement will get you in trouble. Self-awareness and hard work will earn you the access and opportunities you desire. They will also lead you to the next logical step on your career journey, if you patiently let them.

The self-evaluation process is crucial in your transition from student of the performing arts to professional performing artist.

It does not matter at what age you make this transition. Maybe it is not a transition from school. Maybe it is a transition from one career to another. What matters is that, whether you are transitioning at 22 or 42 or 62, you think about who you are and where you realistically want to be and that your action plan accurately and honestly reflects the results of this self-examination.

That you were once the star of the school's musicals does not mean much to a professional casting director in terms of credits. But your training, along with the experience, exposure and confidence you gained from doing it, certainly does matter. Because you were a star in high school or college is not reason enough to cast you into a series lead role two weeks after graduation, although I have met many young actors who have disagreed.

This is a tough realization in the transition for a lot of students who have achieved notoriety while at school. I admit that the humbling part of the transition can be painful. But it is also extremely necessary. It is one thing to know you have talent that matters and is meaningful. It is another thing to behave that way.

Let your previous experience show through in your preparation and your auditions for professional projects. Your ability to have a level of comfort in an audition situation or on a stage that is the result of your having appeared in college and/or other local productions can work in your favor, if you let it.

It may sound like I am asking you to completely start over, but

I am not. Look at this new perspective you will have on yourself as the result of the first of many such self-evaluations you should undertake throughout your professional career.

Start by cleaning your emotional house a bit. Take stock of what you have. Keep what can be helpful to you along the way and throw out the rest.

You will meet a lot of interesting people along your journey. Most you will really like. Some you will loathe. It is important to learn how to properly process the professional experiences you will have in the business. I wish I could tell you that all casting directors are wonderful folks, that all agents are great people and that all managers are kind and nurturing. They are not. But I can assure you that most are.

Remember, sometimes initial perceptions can be misleading, especially negative ones. Do not let a sense of entitlement or your own perceptions stand in the way of the positive experiences that await you in the development of your career.

One of the most important skills you will need to develop in your transition is the ability to hear and see things only in terms of black and white, instead of in the vibrant colors that actors tend to paint onto and into most of their experiences. It is important to look at things the way they really are, objectively, not the way you may emotionally spin them to be. This applies to your interactions with people, too.

For example, your default should not be to assume that a certain casting director hated you because he was not terribly friendly to you at an audition. Perhaps that is just the way he operates when he does business.

Unless you have previously given someone a reason to dislike you, do not take what you perceive to be his or her negative behavior toward you personally. It is not that the casting director liked you or did not like you, or that you are too fat or too thin or too short or too tall, that will or will not get you the part.

Most of the time, it will just be that they hired someone else. Black and white. Yes or no. No gray area whatsoever.

When I call a casting director to follow up on how a client's audition went, the answer I hear most often (which is the answer I hate the most) is, "They went another way." They went another way? What does that mean? I am not even sure *they* know.

So while my client may have been liked or disliked, too fat or too thin, too short or too tall, ultimately it is not about any of those things that really matter. They either got the job or they did not. Period. Black and white. It would do them no good to beat themselves up over it. Given that "they went another way," there is nothing the actor could have done that would have made any difference. There rarely is.

More importantly, the audition process is not about getting a part (or not), but it is in this overall process where you can impact the bigger picture of your career. You will read about how to accomplish that goal later in the book.

Successful transition is the result of successful focus. Do not rush your transition. Let it happen. Learn from every incident, accident and happy discovery along the way.

I talk a lot about one's journey because your career needs to be in constant movement, always a work in progress. Seeing it as a journey will prevent you from just running in place and from ever feeling as though you are stuck.

Looking at your career development as a journey will always keep you in forward movement. That is why an action plan is crucial. Like a road map, it will help get you where you are going, regardless of the rest stops you take along the way.

Learn to use what you know from the past to help you mold and plan for your future. Learn to trust your judgment. Never doubt your faith in your ability to succeed. Remember to take those occasional, but regular, rest stops for some self-awareness, reflection and personal evaluation.

Take care of business and the rest will fall into place, in its own time, not yours. Transition yourself by being prepared to handle whatever is around the next corner. Learn to recognize and value the small successes you will achieve each day along your career journey.

CHAPTER 2

SKILLS TO BUILD A CAREER ON IN THE NEW LANDSCAPE

I N *The Business of Acting: Learn the Skills You Need to Build the Career You Want*, I introduce readers to the four categories of critical skills that every actor must acquire to chart and maintain a successful career journey. They are the building blocks for everything else that follows, both in the book and on your career journey.

The same holds true in this book. In order to create and launch an action plan for career success in the new business of acting, you must understand, customize and build on these skills to keep you professionally challenged, personally motivated, emotionally fit and always prepared for the opportunities you will create. It is about empowerment and proactivity in the process, with no room whatsoever for an entitled attitude that will quickly derail any progress you may have been fortunate enough to make.

I have seen first-hand the significant differences and the marked advantages learning and implementing these skills can have on one's approach, attitude and day-to-day process and progress. I have also seen first-hand some of the devastating disappointment that can come from not being focused, not being prepared and not being smart in how you handle the business of your career.

They were vitally important to introduce in the first book. They are even more important to revisit now.

These four skills categories are:

+ Behavior
+ Communication
+ Awareness
+ Perception

Now, let's look at each category individually, in terms of what it means, how it works and why it matters.

BEHAVIOR SKILLS

How you behave, the attitude you display and how you respond in and to personal and professional situations says a lot about the kind of person you are and about the kind of actor you will be to work with. You will see that negative behavior can stand between an actor and an opportunity. You will also discover that positive behavior can land you an opportunity that can easily pass over someone else whose behavior is questionable. But, first, you have to be able to recognize and assess your own behavior and come to terms with whether or not your responses to certain situations are appropriate or inappropriate—helpful to you or harmful to you.

You will see that sometimes it is easy to engage in negative behavior without being aware of it. That is why developing keen self-awareness skills is so important to this process.

Inappropriate behavior, a bad attitude or any sense of entitlement toward what you seek to achieve will eventually, if not quickly, create the kind of reputation that will be tough to overcome, even if or when you ever outgrow the phase that got you into trouble in the first place.

While I was writing my first book, I spent almost two years undercover as an actor, in between my professional and personal day-to-day activities and responsibilities. It was quite an eye-opening experience that taught me that no matter how talented, how prepared or how right someone was for a part, their attitude, their interactions, or their over-confidence (or lack of confidence) can easily get them categorized as uncastable.

For the former working actor who suddenly stops getting called in to audition when once auditions were as routine as they should be—and wonders why or what happened—the answer generally lies in one of three scenarios: 1) the actor has stopped taking auditions seriously and, as a result, gives off an attitude of being uncooperative that sends the casting director the message not to bring them in again, that they are not worth the effort; 2) the actor does not think he needs to study or train any longer and, as a result, gets rusty and, quite frankly, bad at auditioning; or 3) the actor has become such a pain in the ass to their agent and/or manager that whoever is representing him has given up and stopped submitting him altogether just so they can avoid having to deal with him under any circumstances.

For the young and/or new-to-the-business actor, it is usually naiveté that is the killer of opportunity. Thinking that all you have to do is walk in, look the part, be charming and the role will be yours will get you nothing. Schools need to get better at teaching students of the performing arts how to excel at auditions, not just at acting.

While there are many, many excellent teachers and classes in the professional landscape, academic courses are more focused on education for grade's and degree's sake and not on the skills and tools an actor really needs to stay out of behavior trouble and actually land an acting job.

It is important to recognize and accept that when you first enter the business of acting, regardless of the previous (academic) education you have, you are still required to learn the skills you will need to audition and to book a role. Not understanding this—or refusing to believe that this could apply to you, can generate the kind of behavior in young and new-to-the-business actors that screams "novice," "amateur," "unprofessional"—three labels you need to work hard to avoid ever having tagged on you, *ever* (and especially), if you are at the very beginning of your journey.

At any point in your career, bad behavior will get you noticed for all of the wrong reasons.

COMMUNICATION SKILLS

How you say what you say can often be far more significant than the contents of the message itself. Learning how to communicate effectively is a key skill lacking in far too many people. This applies to both your verbal and written communications, as well as to what your body language is saying for you and about you. Most actors have no trouble saying what they want to say, but packaging their words appropriately is a skill many have not yet learned. It is a skill you must master.

Honing your communication skills also includes perfecting your listening skills. Listening should be at least 50 percent of your interaction with others. Whether in an audition situation or on a set, your ability to both listen to and to hear what is being directed at you can make a significant difference in your ability to succeed.

Listening is about taking direction. Listening is also about taking time to stop and learn.

Asking for what we want has also become a challenge these days. Many of us have become so lazy, so bad and so sloppy at communicating in this new landscape that it is almost laughable, if it were not so potentially harmful to how we are perceived. More about that shortly.

Text messaging and IM shorthand do not substitute for acceptable business correspondence. These tools of the new landscape have, without a doubt, made doing business and staying on top of business possible and effective in ways we could not have imagined before. But they have also changed the acceptable playing field.

Texting has taken the place of a lot of actual person-to-person conversation among at least one generation. This is unfortunate. How can you really connect with someone without really "connecting" to him or her? Sometimes it is okay, and even preferable, to pick up the phone, call the person you want to reach and actually talk with them.

Learning and adapting communications skills for the new business of acting includes both using the new tools wisely *and* not leaving the traditional, proven, effective means of communication behind.

If you are seeking representation, it is not okay to contact a prospective agent or manager by text messaging them or by infiltrating their Facebook page, LinkedIn profile, Twitter or other account. It has happened to me. If you want to make me aware of who you are, if you want me to consider a meeting with you about representation, if you want me to attend a showcase or play you are in, go to our website and find out about my preferred methods of contact—and, perhaps to your surprise, you will discover that sometimes I will, actually, still like getting mail that the postman, not my Internet service provider, delivers.

I know that I am not alone. Agents, managers and casting directors get hundreds of e-mails a day. Do not inundate us further with trying to get an audition or a meeting this way. It is much easier to hit "delete" than it is to deal with a real letter. At least it is for me.

Recognize that you will be judged by your communication skills. If you mishandle that significant piece of your business, you will make it too easy for us to not take you seriously and to dismiss your inquiry. Every outreach attempt you make can have either a consequence or a benefit generated from it that can have an impact on your career journey.

Awareness Skills

Self-awareness will get you in touch and keep you in touch with who you are and how you feel. Awareness of the people, circumstances and environment around you can keep your behavior an asset to your career.

Self-awareness is about being sensitive to situations around you all the time. Self-awareness is also about being able to size up a situation in order to gauge your appropriate next step. What is the mood around you in the casting office? What is the mood on the set where you are working? Learn to be aware of your own presence in the presence of others.

Learn to be aware of the activity around you. Let this awareness work for you.

A former student of mine in The Business of Acting class was eager, very early in the semester, to tell me that she had, through much effort on her part, snagged an interview with a respected talent agent about representation. I was quick to let her know that I thought that it was too early in the process for her to be seeking anything but an informational interview from this person (more about that in Chapter 10), but she was particularly insistent that she was more than capable of going to this meeting and handling herself in a professional manner.

Her appointment was scheduled for the following day and if I could not talk her out of her approach, I was eager, if not cautiously hesitant, to hear about how it all went.

The next week when I saw her in class, she was not her usually perky, outgoing self. I asked her about what had transpired at her highly anticipated meeting.

She went on to tell me about the difficulty she had (and, later, the inflated price she paid) to find a place to park when she arrived at the high rise office building on the west side of Los Angeles, where the agency was located. She explained that while she thought she had allowed enough time to get there, the traffic was (and it always is) awful and after (and because of) the parking space fiasco, she arrived about ten minutes late for her appointment.

The receptionist asked her to take a seat in the waiting area while the agent she was scheduled to see was alerted that she had arrived. The student took a seat and nervously began thumbing through some recent issues of *Daily Variety* while she waited. After about five minutes, a piercing alarm sounded in the building.

Calmly, but quickly, everyone from inside the office began exiting the suite and leaving the building, including the receptionist, but the student sat there, continuing to flip through *Daily Variety*, pretending not to notice the activity around her.

Finally, a person who looked like an executive came from an

office within the suite and walked through the reception area on her way out of the building. The excutive was surprised to see someone sitting in the waiting area.

The executive stopped to tell the student that the fire alarm, which continued to blare loudly, meant that everyone had to evacuate the building immediately, to which the student responded, "It took me three months to get the meeting I'm here for and I'm not leaving until that happens."

The executive reached for her cell phone, made a call and watched a minute later as the student was escorted out of the waiting area (and, soon after, the building), by two security guards.

As the student's entitled attitude would later prove, she lost out on more than just a meeting; she destroyed both a potential opportunity and a valuable connection.

Did I mention that the executive who she gave attitude to turned out to be the agent she was scheduled to meet with?

Do you think that meeting ever got rescheduled?

Awareness of where you are, what is appropriate for where you are and how to respond to whatever happens around you wherever you are can make or break a career opportunity.

PERCEPTION SKILLS

How you perceive others and how others perceive you can significantly stand in the way of your career or significantly help move it along. For our purposes, perception is the initial feeling we get, the first impression we form, of or about someone upon our first experience with them. No matter how strongly someone else might tell you differently about that person, our perceptions, once formed, are difficult, if not impossible, to change.

If the first time we meet I find you to be pushy, demanding and difficult, that is an impression I am going to carry with me for a long time. I certainly would not be eager for a repeat visit. If, on the other hand, I find you to be warm, friendly and pleasant, you can bet that is an encounter I will want to repeat.

You can imagine how this might play itself out in an audition situation where you are meeting a casting director for the first time or when you are meeting for the first time with a potential agent or manager.

Yes, you will form an immediate impression of everyone you meet, but remember that they are also forming an immediate impression of *you*.

Clearly, I wish that the student who screwed herself out of the agent meeting she had scheduled had first read *The Business of Acting* before heading to that appointment.

Before we move on, it is essential that we address how the impact of life in cyberspace has given new meaning to and magnified the importance of understanding and avoiding the significant damage that can inadvertently be caused by stupidly, boldly going where generations of actors (and others) have never been able to go before—the Internet.

For all of the advantages the World Wide Web has given us, it has also created some danger zones when it comes to creating and launching an action plan for career success in any field. I have been exploring this issue in my academic classes, and the lessons from those discussions are an important part of this discourse.

Social media, if not used smartly and strategically, can ruin your chances at landing the opportunities you seek and deserve. It becomes easy to overlook the fact that anything you upload or otherwise publish on Facebook, MySpace, Twitter, YouTube, your own blog or Web page—or a comment you make on someone else's posting—has the potential to be seen by a planet full of online readers beyond just the few thousand cyber friends or followers you may have amassed.

While this is not new news, what is important to focus on is the trend for everyone from college admissions directors to prospective employers to check you out online in their process of evaluating your candidacy for everything from a place in the freshman class, to your admission to graduate school, to your acceptance for a volunteer position or internship, to your being hired for a paying job, or your being taken on as a client.

Most agents and managers I know routinely perform a Google search of their current clients' names to see what has been written about them or what they might have written about themselves that appears somewhere online. Many of us routinely monitor our clients' profiles and credit listings on professional resource sites like IMDb.com to ensure the accuracy of those listings. Many of us also check out potential clients on the Web to see what has been said about them, but, more importantly, what they have said—and are saying—about themselves on their own social media pages, blogs and personal websites—and here is where you can get yourself in trouble.

Later, we will discuss the rules and regulations of work confidentiality when it comes to posting information on the Web about acting jobs you land, but, for now, let's focus on how what you post can negatively impact you and your brand—and how to avoid that from happening.

Be careful about the comments you make about other people (online, in a conversation, on your cell phone—anywhere that is public and where anything you say or anything you write can be overheard or read by anyone). Do not be negative. Do not be nasty. Do not be personal.

If you are annoyed with your agent because she has not returned your call in four days, do not Tweet about it. If you feel that you were poorly treated at an audition, do not write about it on your Facebook page. If you think the actor who got the role you went in for will not be as good as you would have been, do not blog about it. Do you sense the trend here?

As a business, as a brand, you are expected to protect that brand as you grow your business. Coke may think that it is better than Pepsi, but you will not find anything negative about Pepsi written anywhere (publicly, at least) by Coke, or vice versa. Think like a businessperson; think like a publicist. In short, think before you write or post anything. In a world where anything you post is instantly, globally public, it is too risky a proposition to think that you can later take back or delete anything from even temporary existence after the fact without a potential consequence at some level.

Yes, opinions will be made and perceptions sealed about you by both the kind of person you are and the kind of person you (virtually) appear to be.

Be smart about how you want to be perceived by others and honor the integrity of your brand in all that you do.

CHAPTER 3

THE ART OF THE HEAD SHOT:

A Picture Is Worth a Thousand Words and a Potential Opportunity

B Y FAR, THE greatest number of inquiries I get from actors through my Business of Acting Blog and during my workshops, seminars and classes, are questions about head shots—and with good reason.

Your head shot is the single most important tool in your actor's tool kit. The right one can open doors to opportunity; a bad shot can eliminate you from the running before you even get out of the gate.

The old saying goes that a picture is worth a thousand words, and while that adage was not intended to apply to actors' head shots, I cannot think of a better way to help me make a critical point: the issue of perception—how you are perceived by others—is never potentially more harmful or potentially more beneficial to you than in your photo.

Many, many more people will see your head shot than you will ever meet in person—hundreds, thousands, maybe more. How you decide to let the world see you says a lot about who you are and how you feel about your talent, your skills, your brand and your potential for success in this business.

If ever there have been changes in the new business of acting landscape, there have been no greater changes than in the business of and the importance of head shots.

When *The Business of Acting* was first published in 2002, the state of the art was black and white, three-quarter "head" (really head and body) shots. Actors and those of us who represent them made most of our casting submissions by sending hard copy 8 x 10 photos with resumes printed on the back. Actors spent lots of money printing (usually) one hundred copies at a time of their (usually) single head shot, and agents and managers then spent more money mailing or messengering envelopes with clients' photos to casting offices all over town.

It was a good time to be in the business of head shot reproductions. Professional photo labs could hardly keep up with photographers' needs and demands for developing film and printing proof sheets, not to mention the ongoing demand from actors and those of us who represented them at that time for hard copies of those perfect black and white, single head shots with which submissions were made and auditions sought.

There was not much opportunity then for actors to legitimately self-submit, but when there was, they also used hard copies of their head shots to mail in to casting directors who sought submissions from actors mostly through casting ads in industry-established and recognized hard-copy sources such as *Back Stage*, in New York, and *Back Stage West*, in Los Angeles.

Today, at least as of this writing, one national edition of *Back Stage* serves actors on both coasts and the online presence and availability of this formerly just hard-copy publication and the creation and addition of other legitimate online self-submission services, including ActorsAccess.com and CastingNetworks.com, has made it possible for actors to get their names, their faces and their resumes in front of the eyes of casting directors in legitimate ways that just a few years ago would have been thought impossible.

The post office has lost a lot of money that was formerly spent by actors on stamp purchases to mail photos and other self-promotional materials. Many a delivery service has shuttered since the click of a button has replaced the need for talent representatives to incur the costs of getting hard copy materials of clients to casting offices. Not even the fastest messenger service could beat the speed (instant) and the cost (free) of an online electronic submission.

The technology has, indeed, given actors everywhere a proactive and empowering edge in marketing their brand, but it has also changed the playing field in other ways, specifically where head shots are concerned.

Black and white shots as the norm have been replaced by the now requisite color image. The three-quarter head/body shot has been replaced by the now (as of this writing), requisite just-head shot. Pushing this particular change are the now requisite demands that come with the technology.

With the submission of hard copy, 8 x 10 photos the rare occurrence now, most casting directors for most projects are opening thumbnail photo files instead of large mailing envelopes. Instead of studying a single head shot at a time held in their hand, casting directors are now looking at a sea of thumbnail photos on their computer screens from which to decide who to call in for an audition—or not.

What makes a head shot photo "pop" off the hard copy printed page is a completely different set of criteria than what makes a thumbnail jump out at the viewer when scanned quickly among many others.

It is all about the eyes—and, now, it is also all about diversity and versatility. The one perfect head shot that all actors needed that I wrote about in my first book has been replaced by the need for *multiple* perfect, customized shots, particularly for submissions for commercials, but still important for theatrical casting use, as well.

Because a snap judgment decision is made by a casting director about whether to audition an actor based on the casting director's perception of that actor from just their thumbnail image, it is critical that that image be spot on, which has created the need among agents and managers to have a variety of looks in their clients' profiles that are all available for submission use.

The online casting services have made it easy and relatively cheap for actors to upload many different photos and this is a great thing for all concerned.

While you should make hard copy prints of one of your photos (you will, in most cases, still be asked to bring a photo/resume with you to an audition and those who represent you might still want to have a few hard copy photos on hand for that rare occasion when a casting director is not accepting electronic submissions), most of the photos contained in your online profile for submissions will never see a sheet of photo paper.

When it comes time for you to print your photos, do so in small batches. The need for printing one hundred at a time has passed, unless you are auditioning ten times a week, which few (if any) actors are.

While the technology has changed, the basic rules of how to ensure you book a head shot session that succeeds in every way have remained exactly the same. There are important rules and guidelines to follow to help you navigate through the maze of people who call themselves photographers versus those professionals who, indeed, focus on the business at hand.

The new business of acting is full of people seeking to make a few extra bucks with their auto-focus, digital cameras and a never-ending pool of actors seeking to get head shots on the cheap. The mistake both make is bad business for both.

A professional photographer has an eye and an art for the work he does. Not seeking out a professional head shot photographer for your head shot session is myopic, miserly and foolish. Not investing in the single most important component of your career is counter-strategic and con-active (my word, as opposed to proactive). You may think that you are saving money by having a friend or a friend-of-a-friend do you a favor and take your pictures, but making that choice will cost you.

It is not acceptable to justify that decision by telling yourself that that photo will do "for now." Would you want your auto mechanic to put tires on your car that will do "for now"? I hope not.

Let's get into the nuts and bolts and whys and why-nots. It is all about opening doors and creating opportunity. One of the biggest mistakes actors make, particularly young and new-to-the-business actors, is in not understanding the importance of their head shot in launching their action plan, introducing their brand and in building their careers.

Older actors are often guilty, too, when they continue to use head shots taken years ago that no longer look like them. This is just as effective in derailing the career of an actor with credits as it is in preventing the new actor in his attempts to build his resume.

Whether by e-mail or snail mail, I get hundreds of unsolicited head shots a month from actors seeking representation. I wish I could share some of them with you. These images would help me make my point quite easily and clearly. They are horrible pictures of people who probably are not as horrible as their pictures make them appear or that they are perceived to be. But you never know.

Like most agents, managers and casting directors, I do not often have the luxury of time to sit, stare at and analyze every photo that is sent in by every actor seeking representation or a general meeting. Instead, in just a quick second, we will see enough of the picture to form a perception, a first impression, of the person in the photo. Short as it is, it is enough time for us to make a business decision about him or her.

Agents, managers and casting directors all look at photos quickly and just as quickly form opinions about whether the actor pictured warrants a second, longer look. If not, the photo gets tossed or the JPEG gets deleted.

Whether these initial reactions and responses are fair or accurate is not the issue. The issue is that in just a second someone whose attention you are trying to capture will make a decision about you based on a first impression, not (necessarily) based on reality.

How you are instantly perceived makes the critical difference between who gets to the next step with this agent, manager or casting director and who does not. There is an awful lot riding on this one quick look.

It is *all* about perception. What the image in your photo reveals about you is vital. This image can help open doors to opportunity or it can shut you out—all based on a quick look.

If you send me a photo of yourself that reveals too much skin or too many muscles or overly flaunts some other trait or body part that you deem important for me to notice, you bet I will notice it. I will notice that one trait that you have decided to magnify and showcase, rather than get a general, overall look at what should be the complete, real you. Instead, you will have me stuck on those muscles, that navel, that cleavage, that tattoo. Get the picture?

Too many actors' head shots do not get the attention or the serious consideration that they might deserve from potential agents, managers or casting directors because the actors have forced the recipient to look at them as a particular type, rather than as a real person with potential and intrigue. In the new business of acting, "brand" is the new "type" and it is only the carefully, strategically marketed brand that will find a repeat audience upon which to make its mark and build a relationship with.

This says a lot about how you see yourself, how you feel about yourself and about how you choose to be seen by others. Most actors, if given the opportunity to understand how critical this is, would never choose to send out the images of themselves that many do send.

Let me emphasize that I recognize the need to be noticed. Let me also emphasize that getting noticed should be about generating a positive reaction, not an inaccurate, negative response. You want to get recipients to turn your picture over, to look at your resume and then to give you fair consideration for an audition or for a general meeting. Give them that opportunity. Give yourself that opportunity. If you want that meeting, if you want that audition, do not run the risk of not having your talent seen at all because you have chosen a photo that sends the wrong message about who you are.

What makes a great head shot? That is not as easy to answer as what makes a bad one. Your head shot is your calling card, your business card. It is meant to introduce you to a tremendous number of people who may be able to use your services when the right opportunity comes along.

This may sound a bit unnecessary, but it needs to be said anyway: your head shot should look like *you*, not like you *think* you should look, but how you *really* look—with all of your characteristics, all of your heart, all of your humanity, all of your sincerity.

You should be wearing clothes that are really the clothes you wear in your everyday life, not a new outfit that you buy for the photo session or an old suit that you have not worn in years just to achieve "a look." If you have not lived in the clothes you select to wear for your photo session, a sense of not being comfortable in your own skin will come across in your photos.

There is a variety of looks you will need to capture in a single photo session. Achieve these looks with an attitude, not an outfit. The essence of any character you will play, like the very essence of you, is not in the clothes you wear, but in the person you are. Let that person shine through in your photos.

Do not enter any photo session with your mind already made up about what you want the end result to look like.

Predetermined notions about what you should look like in your new photos, what you should wear, how you should be lit and how you should pose are not decisions for you to make by yourself. In most cases, they are not decisions you should be involved with making at all.

Leave the artistic elements of your session for the photo artist you have hired to deal with. A successful photo session is the result of a successful collaboration, but it is important to bow to the experience of the person behind the camera who will enter every session with a greater subjective point of view about how to achieve the desired results than almost anyone facing the lens from the front.

What makes for a really good head shot? In a word, it is when the photo pops off the screen or off the page, when it is striking for all of the right reasons.

How much you pay for your photo session has absolutely nothing to do with the quality of what you will get from it. Any photographer who tells you differently is not a photographer you should be doing business with.

Your head shot session is about two things: you and your photographer. You have to be comfortable with him or her. He or she has to be comfortable with you. It should never be about the money.

I have known actors who have spent up to $5,000 on a single photo session with a highly reputed photographer, only to become so intimidated by that photographer that most of the shots revealed a look of near-fright on their faces. That look could be the result of intimidation or fright—or the realization, halfway through the session, that they actually paid that much money to sit there and be told how to pose.

I know a lot of great photographers who charge a variety of fees for the artistic and creative services they provide. What you pay for your professional session will not affect the outcome or the quality of your shoot as much as the level of comfort you feel in the presence of the person taking your pictures. It is that level of comfort, not dollars, that makes great pictures. If you have the money and feel comfortable with a higher-priced photographer, then use him or her, but most actors do not have that luxury—and most do not need it.

You can take a look at a selection of head shots I really like and the photographers who took them at TheBusinessOfActing.com.

How do you find one of these remarkable artists? Start by looking at the head shots of everyone you know and anyone else you can. Ask around. Ask your friends, ask their friends and ask other actors you meet in classes and at auditions (but only *after* you both have auditioned; more about the rules of the waiting room in Chapter 5).

Do you like what you see in their photos, not just how they look, but how they look like they *feel* and how they make *you* feel? Do they look comfortable? Are their photos pleasant to your eye? Does your eye see the overall photo in general or something specific in it?

If your eyes go to the eyes of the person in the picture first, it is a great head shot. If your eye, instead, goes to an item of clothing, an earring or exposed skin first, then you are looking at a photo that does not serve the subject well. If the viewer is looking at anything but your face, the photo is not working.

When you see work you like, get that photographer's name and contact information. Call and make an appointment to meet with him. Look at a portfolio of the photographer's work (the good ones will be more than happy to let you have a look; in fact, they will most likely insist on it) and discuss prices. Do this with three or four different photographers.

When all of your criteria have been met, you will have found a comfortable match and a great photographer who is meant to take your head shots.

How much should you spend, really, and what is a reasonable range of prices? I have seen terrific head shots taken by artful, professional photographers who charge (as of this writing) in the $350 to $500 range.

Be clear on what your session fee buys you. In the new business of acting, this should include all of the shots taken given to you on a CD. It should also include an agreement on the number of shots you can select from your session that the photographer will clean up and color correct in PhotoShop (or similar program) in his process of resizing and preparing these new "master" shots for you to print or upload directly to an online service. You should expect to be given these as JPG or TIFF (or similar) digital files on a new "master" CD.

It is not unusual for a professional photographer to include these services for one shot from each setup or look; additional shots would be prepared for you for an additional cost. Be clear on what you are getting for the price you are paying and what any additional services you might want or need (now or later) will cost.

One photo session should last you at least a year, as long as you do not do anything significant to change your look after your photos have been taken. Remember, you must look in person as you look in your head shot, within reason, all the time—the same general haircut and style, the same approximate weight, the same overall appearance.

I am not saying you cannot change how you look. What I am saying is that if you do decide to change your appearance (or if living your life has somehow changed your appearance for you), then schedule a new photo session.

Nothing will damage your opportunity for an acting job quicker than if a casting director calls you in for an audition based on how you look in the head shot submitted to her and you come through the door looking like someone else entirely. Do not let that happen, ever.

Here is another "do not let happen, ever": never ask for or let any photo of you be so cleaned up that you become ageless. Got a new blemish on your face that has suddenly appeared the morning of your head shot session? It is okay to get rid of it in PhotoShop. Got a funny-looking ear, double chin or noticeable mole? Leave it alone. Let that mole show. Let those lifelines show. They are part of the essence of you. The pimple is a temporary annoyance; the rest stays with you, so it also stays visible in your photos.

Get proper rest the night before your session. Go to bed after lunch if necessary! Eat a no-salt or low-sodium diet for the few days prior to your session. Too many actors as they age, both men and women, have this thing about not wanting to let their age show in their photos. Remember: look the way you really look. Be proud of any facial lines and other distinguishing facial characteristics that you were born with or have earned. Let your individuality come through in your head shots.

Who should pick the photos that will help establish your brand? Not you.

If you are represented, your agent (theatrical and/or commercial) and manager will want to choose what tools they have available to market you with. Let them. While you may disagree with their choice or choices of head shots to use, they will always be making these decisions with an eye toward what is needed, subjectively, to get the job done.

Often, there will be discrepancies between your agents (theatrical and commercial) and your manager (if you have one) over what they each think represents you best. It is all personal choice, so let them have it and give them what they need and what they want to do the work you have retained them to do.

If you are not yet represented, ask people you know, and especially people who do not know you well, for their opinions of your photos. Someone who knows you well will more than likely try to find the you they know in your head shot, while someone who is not terribly familiar with you will be more apt to look at your photos the way a casting director or talent representative who does not know you might look at them for the first time, thus picking out the shot (or shots) that give him or her the best feeling about which photo they *perceive* captures the real you.

While you should not choose your own photos, you must, nonetheless, be comfortable with the choice or choices suggested by others and the selection or selections ultimately made. After all, you are the both the product and the brand and it is you, not any of the people who may have selected your photo or photos, who will be walking into a business meeting set up as a result of this image selected and submitted.

When printing hard copy head shots to bring to auditions with you, it is essential to have your name printed on the front (usually bottom, usually centered). While your name will, of course, be on the back of your photo on your resume, should the resume ever become separated from the photo (unless you print your resume directly onto the back of your photos as you need them, which is what I highly recommend and is what we do in my office), your identity will still be known.

Once you have the CD with the master images of your perfect head shots, take it to a processing lab that specializes in printing and duplicating head shots for actors.

Digital litho reproductions are the way to go for crisp, clean, true copies of the master shot or shots you decide to (or are asked to) print hard copies of. Like photographers, reproduction labs and services come in all cost and quality varieties. After all of the time and energy (and dollars) you will have invested in your career to get those perfect head shots, do not compromise on that quality by accepting cheap copies of great originals that will not serve you.

Research the labs in your area. Look at samples of their work, look at the reproductions your actor friends have, and then make a smart decision that works for you.

While the technology has changed and will continue to evolve, what will remain a constant through the implementation of both your action plan and the growth of your career is the need for you to have nothing less than the best tools with which to build your career. Do not be penny wise and pound foolish. It is better to wait a little bit longer for a great session you can afford than to rush the process at a bargain price that will not have saved you anything in the long run.

In short, do not be cheap. Evoke The Business of Acting Gift Registry® concept (that will be introduced on page 136), if necessary, to help you fund this number one need.

CHAPTER 4

THE BUSINESS OF TALENT REPRESENTATION:

A Perspective on the New Landscape

TECHNOLOGY and an actor's ability and opportunity to self-submit on roles being cast have, indeed, redefined the new business of acting from a casting director's perspective. But the landscape has been equally, if not more so, redefined by the sea of changes, both in attitude and expectation, in the business of talent representation.

Much has changed in this area since my first book was published. Back in the early 2000's, there was much concern over the need for informing and warning actors about how not to get scammed by talent representatives. Today, the concern is more about informing talent representatives, specifically, managers, how not to get scammed by actors.

The laws have not changed yet (at least as of this writing), but the playing field certainly has.

We are in an industry where there are many more actors who seek representation than there are agents and agencies to represent them. This has given rise, in the last decade, in particular, to a new breed of talent managers who have also attracted to their rosters a new kind of actor.

In the State of California, it is illegal for a talent manager to seek, to procure and/or to negotiate work for a client. Those tasks have been left, legally, to the domain of talent agents, who are licensed and bonded and expected to perform due diligence in the representation of any client.

Since 2002, there has been a movement underway, largely spearheaded by talent manager Rick Siegel, who learned the hard way, that while the laws were busy protecting actors, there were managers who were in need of legal protection of their own and finding that none was available. In fact, as the laws currently stand, the system pretty much assumes that any manager who is doing the job a client has hired them to do is breaking the law.

There is a four-part interview with Siegel in our *Inside the Business of Acting* Web TV series (at InsideTheBusinessOfActing .com). It is vital viewing for additional information and actor-specific advice on this topic.

Actors (as well as writers, producers, directors and others) retain representation to help them grow their careers. Agents are authorized by law, and by their clients, to submit and pitch them for all appropriate work opportunities. Managers, on the other hand, have always legally had their hands tied. Prevented by law (in the State of California) from doing any of this, managers are legally limited to advising, guiding and counseling a client in their career development, but must work in tandem with the agent who also represents the client in order to be in a safety zone for engaging in these other activities.

With an agent in place, the system assumes that a safety net is also in place for the actor. The system assumes that managers are not possibly capable of doing the job without the permission of a legally sanctioned agent. How ridiculous. This assumes that all agents are ethical and that all managers, if given the opportunity, will screw a client.

This assumption is rooted in the need for agents to be licensed before they can practice their craft and that there are no official requirements, at present, for managers to meet before calling themselves managers. This is a huge problem both for the legitimate talent management community and actors alike.

Since anyone can call themselves a manager, the field is wide open for the unscrupulous businessperson (and I use that term loosely) to open an office, rent some furniture, attend some talent showcases and/or otherwise "discover" talent, sign them to long-term contracts and charge them outrageous commission rates and other fees.

Actors get drawn into scams like this all the time, even actors who should know better—and it does not just happen in Los Angeles or New York. There have been plenty of complaints filed and lawsuits pursued in cities all over the country against companies or individuals who claim that they can make you or your kid a star, at the right price. Shame on all of them.

Legitimate talent managers fight this image all the time. The seemingly simple solution would be to require all talent representatives to meet the same requirements to represent talent that agents have to meet. While the process would, no doubt, add to the cost of opening, operating and maintaining a talent management business, it seems that it would be a small price to pay for both peace of mind for clients and a level of protection for managers.

Without these safeguards in place for both actors and managers, problems will—and have—ensued and at a great sacrifice for many a legitimate manager seeking to claim what is rightfully his.

Case in point is the many legal battles that have been waged in the California courts and at the California State Labor Relations Commission pitting formerly happy and content managers against former equally happy and content clients over money.

When an actor signs with (or hires) an agent or a manager to represent him, he is entering into a contract (oftentimes written, sometimes only verbal, but equally as binding) that buys him a business relationship for a kind of pay-as-you-go service.

Agents and managers work as hard as they can to uncover, discover, create, submit, pitch and secure opportunities for their clients all day long. If an agent or manager is not interested in doing the work and thus investing in your potential, then she should not sign you and you should not hire her.

A lot of work hours are put into generating even one audition. The odds of even one audition landing any client a paying job are so insignificant that agents (and increasingly managers) in this economic landscape have the need to represent increasingly larger numbers of clients in an attempt to stack the odds in their favor that at least one person they represent is working all of the time.

Agents and managers do not make a dime unless and until a client works. It is a lot of effort for, particularly in the early stages of an actor's career, very little or no compensation, which is why when an actor finally lands a paying gig, commission on that job is expected, required contractually and usually long overdue.

Actors understand this equation when they seek and sign with an agent or a manager—and all are eagerly willing to commit to paying ten percent of their gross earnings to their agent and up to fifteen percent of their gross earnings to their manager; that is, until it is time to pay on these promises.

Manager Rick Siegel's war against the ungrateful, unappreciative and cheap actor began when a client of his refused to pay commissions due him for his work on her behalf. As Siegel began his own legal battle against this client and against the system that still makes it possible for an actor to steal commissions from their manager, many other managers who were also ripped off by now former clients began coming forward.

It was becoming clear that there was beginning to be a potential epidemic of sorts spreading through the actor community that infected some artists with the idea that it was okay, for whatever set of reasons that motivated him or her, to do the equivalent of what, in my opinion, is shoplifting at their manager's place of business. In truth, these actors did nothing legally wrong. All they are guilty of is taking advantage of the current law that allows them to take the actions they have taken. While they have committed no legal wrongdoing or crime in doing so, at its core and at its simplest, it wasn't a very nice thing to do to a manager who seemingly did nothing more than what that actor came to him or her for in the first place.

The public records of court documents include many high profile (and other not so high profile) cases of actor vs. manager and manager vs. actor over commission issues, including Arsenio Hall,[1] Nia Vardalos (of *My Big Fat Greek Wedding* fame),[2] Sean Hayes (from *Will and Grace*),[3] Rosa Blasi (from *Strong Medicine*),[4] Tony Plana (from *Ugly Betty*),[5] Pamela Anderson,[6] Thomas Haden Church,[7] Jason Behr (from *Roswell*),[8] and many others who have taken legal action over commissions, to the tune of millions of dollars.

According to the National Conference of Personal Managers,

over the last forty years, the State Labor Commission has voided an estimated $250 million in personal management commissions.[9]

This becomes an issue for some actors who have achieved the career and financial success for which they sought out a manager to help create for them. The, usually, young or new-to-the-business actor, is beyond eager to sign with any representative who will take her on and is equally beyond eager to agree to pay them for their work; that is, until she starts earning money.

I do not think that most actors enter into these relationships intending to turn on the very person or company that partners with them to develop, nurture and deliver them to the career they seek, but I do think that two key influencers begin to take shape as the career, for some, does progress: the paycheck factor and the best friend factor.

Let's say you land a regular role on a television series. Let's also say that you are pulling in $1,000 an episode, per week (let's also hope that you will earn more than this amount, but let's work with simple numbers that make the point).

Off the top (unless you are a corporate or other business entity through which you are paid, which is both unlikely and unnecessary in anyone's early career), as a single person, I am told that you would lose about $200 for standard tax withholding. Regardless of what is withheld, your commission to your agent and/or manager is based on the gross amount of your paycheck, which is the amount before the tax withholdings.

Let's say that you are paying your agent the standard ten percent and that you are paying your manager the standard fifteen percent (although some managers will agree to a ten percent commission, in some cases).

In this scenario, from your $1,000 gross payment check, $200 has been withheld for taxes, $100 is due for your agent's commission and then $150 is owed for your management commission, leaving you with a whopping net take-home pay check of $550—almost half of what you earned is gone.

While your related business expenses, including all commissions you pay, will be tax-deductible, it is easy to become fixated on what is going out instead of on what is coming in.

As your frustration from this situation grows (you are working, yes, but you are still finding that you do not really earn enough to get you the things you want), you start talking to your friends, particularly your not-yet-as-successful-as-you actor friends.

Out of these conversations you learn (or are reminded) that it is illegal (in California) for your manager to get you work, and that since your manager actually made it possible for you to get the job to earn the money you are now complaining about not having enough of, perhaps it is time stop paying him at all. Besides, your friends tell you, because you are working regularly on this job that the manager either got you or helped get you, you are too busy to do anything else right now, so what is your manager doing these days except waiting for your checks?

The wheels begin to spin and what was not so long ago tremendous appreciation for the manager agreeing to work with and for you has become a strategic plan hatched to screw your manager out of the payback on the investment he made in you.

Get the picture? It is not a pretty one.

The sad and unfortunate thing here is that there are no winners in this endeavor. While this actor may benefit from seeing a few more dollars in her bank account, one day this job, this series, will end. Who will have been working on her behalf to develop the next opportunity? Certainly not an agent who is, by design, more focused on getting you a paying job than strategizing on and growing the bigger picture of your career. So, you decide to seek out another manager. Really? What manager do you think will take the risk of signing you when you have "a reputation" of not paying what you owe to your previous manager?

It is a small business and it does not take long for this kind of news to spread.

Much money has been spent by managers on attorney fees fighting to get what is rightfully theirs. Many other managers have simply decided to accept the loss and avoid the potentially high costs involved with pursuing these matters. For those who have taken that journey, ultimately, decisions have been made on a case-by-case basis and then are routinely sent to appeal by whichever side lost.

The solution is to create, enact and enforce one law that is applied equally and fairly to all actors who seek and retain managers and all managers who choose to represent them. We can call it the "Honor Your Obligation, Honor Your Commitment Act."

During the writing of my first book, it was managers who were in need of coming with both a warning notice and a list of items to check for any actor seeking to do business with them. Today, it is actors who managers need to be wary of. You seek to grow your business, as we do ours. We each need to be held accountable, responsible and fiscally obligated if any of these relationships are to survive, grow and prosper in the best interests of both a manager's and a client's career.

What makes a great client? Just ask any frustrated agent or manager who spends too much time on the telephone with needy clients, taking away the time from them that they need to do they work that they are hired do, and you will get a short list of concise, but important, requests:

- Do not call just to say "hello."
- Do not call just to see "what's up."
- Do not call to ask about a project a friend went in on that you did not.
- *Do* call if you have something "business important" to discuss. Then get to the point; don't linger, no small talk.
- *Do* ask any and all questions you might have about a scheduled audition.
- *Do* report back (to your manager) on how an audition went.
- *Always* confirm an audition appointment.
- *Always* attempt to accommodate any audition time given to you, unless needing to have it changed (if that is at all possible), is absolutely necessary.
- *Never* show up late for any appointment (your agent or manager does not want to have to take a call from an angry casting director asking about where you are when your audition time has passed).
- *Never* abuse your manager's or agent's e-mail address; use it when you have to and *never* for anything non-business-related.

What makes a great agent or manager? Just ask any frustrated client and they will be quick to tell you the qualifications they seek in the person or people representing them:

- The ability to be reached when really needed.
- Honesty and integrity.

- Passion and compassion.
- The opportunity to learn from them how to become a better actor and more effective in auditions.
- The empathy to understand and support (figuratively, not financially) your desire to succeed and the detours that will inevitably be required along your journey.
- The talent and ability to help you discern your brand.
- An eagerness to see your work when you are performing in a local theatre production and a high interest in watching clips of your work in film and television to both monitor your progress on your journey and to offer constructive feedback (which you need to be open to hearing and discussing).

Impacting both sides and both perspectives is one critical rule of thumb that both talent representatives and clients alike must embrace: managing expectations.

There is a default emotional response among many actors who are convinced that the only thing standing in the way of their having a killer career is the lack of a killer agent and/or manager to open the doors to the opportunities they alone cannot pry open for themselves.

Given this outlook, after the long and often painful search to find, meet and then sign with someone to represent you, it is easy to understand why most actors would then expect that by at least the day after they have signed with an agent or manager, everything will be different, auditions will start pouring in and their long-awaited, eagerly anticipated career will just fall into place.

That, of course, rarely happens, at least not like that. In most cases, what happens in the days, weeks, even months after you sign with any agent or manager is nothing that you will see as physical evidence that anything is any different than it was in your pre-represented (or previously represented) days. How could this happen?

For the lucky some, auditions will be generated quicker than for others. But it all depends. Since you will only know what you are submitted on if/because you are lucky enough to get called in for an audition, you cannot weigh the effort being made on your behalf by only this as a result.

The truth is that, behind the scenes, your agent or manager is busy making all of the appropriate submissions that should be made on your behalf. If you do not trust that this work is, indeed, being done, then you have hired the wrong person to represent you.

Remembering that we who represent you do not earn a dime until you do (actually we would earn our percentage of that dime), then why would we do anything less than everything it takes to generate every appropriate opportunity for both of us?

The managing expectations issue can take its toll on agents and managers, too. Because we know everything that you are submitted on and are not called in for, many of us have to juggle and manage our own emotions over this situation.

I never let a client know what they are submitted on. Doing so would serve no purpose, expect to bruise him or her emotionally about why so many submissions were made and so few (if any) opportunities came for them from those efforts. It is out of your control, as much as it is out of the hands of those who submit you.

It is our job to seek out opportunities and to use the professional tools at our disposal—and our experience—to get you an audition. It is your job to give the best audition possible when those opportunities are generated. It is not a manager's or agent's job to get you a job, just as it is not your job just to land the role you audition for. For you and for the person who represents you, it is about creating and maximizing opportunity.

If your agent or manager makes only smart, strategic submissions on your behalf, it will serve you well. Introducing (or reintroducing) and establishing (or reestablishing) you as a very specific brand and not as an actor who is right for every role and who will audition for anything that comes up, will help to establish and market your brand.

No actor is right for all roles in their specific category. To submit as if you are, or to expect the person who represents you to take this approach on your behalf, is counterproductive.

At the same time, if you recognize that making a great impression is more important than booking a job, that casting director who calls you in will be much more likely to take a pitch on you for another project and more likely to want to audition you again and again. It has to be about your overall career, not about just a single job.

This is the point at which someone will be e-mailing me about managers making submissions for their clients when it is specifically verboten.

That may be the case legally, but managers still do it every day. In fact, when an actor seeks a manager, yes, they should be seeking the special career nurturing and development that the role of manager implies, but they also, in most cases, expect and even insist on the manager's ability to do that additional work.

The legality of managers making submissions or otherwise seeking, procuring and/or negotiating work for their clients is rarely an issue unless and until the client who claims to have been wronged by that manager takes action against him (in California, with the State Labor Relations Commission).

In most cases, that never happens. In most cases, managers and their clients create the kind of effective business partnerships both seek and live pretty much happily ever after—or as long as the relationship has business value for both.

This brings me to a final and equally important item in the business of talent management in the new business of acting: the new and growing field of manager-as-agent.

Given the staggering numbers of people who seek to launch and build their careers as professional actors, and the already professional, working actors seeking to maintain and grow their already-established careers, there are simply too many actors and not enough agents to represent them.

While most actors have agents, far fewer have both agents and managers. A detailed description of the specific differences between the two fields is presented in my first book, *The Business of Acting*, and while the playing field may have changed, those core values have not—and this is where the potential for conflict arises in the new landscape.

In this new environment, because they either cannot secure an agent to represent them, or choose not to, many actors are seeking (and have sought) the services of just a manager, expecting that they will get the same kind of service from a management firm that has long been the sole domain of the talent agency business. This has created a management industry with two different kinds and styles of management.

For managers rooted in the tradition of the work, a small client list is maintained to afford both manager and client the opportunity to develop both the career and the individual talent in an internal non-compete, no-conflict environment. I subscribe to this kind of talent management.

A client list without conflicts among clients (brand, type, age, ethnicity, etc.) makes for a well-rounded and solid roster. On the other hand, talent agencies often have hundreds and hundreds of clients. They have to, just to meet the economic challenges of supporting the infrastructure a business like that requires.

Many managers operate their businesses as I do mine, with a small and diverse client list, a roster that allows us to focus on artists who are on healthy career journeys, affording us the opportunity to spend considerable time investing in careers with potential and careers with longevity. We do a combination of the work we are traditionally expected to do, as well as submit (with or without an agent or agency in place) our clients for consideration to audition and to work.

With regard to the submission piece of this equation, I look at the submissions we generate as, first and foremost, strategic components of a strong and ongoing marketing campaign to get the names, faces and credentials of our clients exposed to a casting director who may or may not know the actor (or who may have forgotten about the actor over time).

Before a submission is meant to generate an audition (which, statistically, it will not), it is meant to create and maintain an awareness of the client and his brand, as a part of the bigger picture of the action plan in place. It can be a highly effective approach.

The new school of talent management that most new, young and some reinvented, experienced managers are subscribing to offers actors less of a hands-on, traditional management approach and more of an agent-submit-only operating model. The availability of this service has risen in a landscape where most actors just want access and want to be both professionally represented and officially submitted.

The argument in the new business of acting has been that if all these managers want to do is keep larger-than-usual-size client lists for a management company and then submit those on the roster as an agent would, then why not just open a talent agency?

The reasons for this are financial, understandable and arguable.

Not creating an agency saves the owner or owners the costs of licensure and the annual costs of having a bond to secure the money they collect and process for their clients. Without any official regulations in place, management companies and managers are avoiding these potentially sizeable expenses. In most locations, all that is required to open your door is a license to do business in the town or city in which you operate.

It is clear that it would be in the best interest of all concerned to make room in this new playing field for some additional game rules that would serve to protect and preserve the integrity of actors seeking careers and the people who they seek out to help them arrive and remain there.

Until we get there, what was true in *The Business of Acting* remains true in *The New Business of Acting*. It is buyer beware in any open marketplace—and that includes the marketplace of talent and those of us who represent them.

CHAPTER 5

THE BUSINESS OF TALENT CASTING
IN THE NEW LANDSCAPE

PICTURE THIS: You are a casting director and have just been handed a script for an episode of a half-hour comedy series with eight guest roles to cast. The problem is that this is a script for an episode that was not scheduled to be produced for a few more weeks. Yet the producers just changed their minds and have moved it up to be shot next week. You have 48 hours or less to issue a breakdown, review submissions, set casting appointments, hold auditions, have callbacks, make deals for the actors to be hired and complete the paperwork.

I won't say that happens under the gun like this every day in the office of every major casting director, but it—or something similar—happens often enough.

Even for a routine casting job, the process can be hectic. In most cases, it takes a special person to do this job without allowing the stress and pressure to give way to near insanity. Script changes, show revisions, network requests, producers' demands, directors' visions, agents' and managers' client sales pitches, actors' behavior— they all have an impact on an ordinary day at the office for a casting director.

These people are much more than creative traffic cops. They are, in many cases, the lifelines of a production.

They can also, however, be perceived as powerful, frightening, unfriendly, rude and uncaring. Notice that I said *perceived,* because, while some casting directors are all of those things some of the time and others are some of those things all of the time, most casting directors are pretty decent, friendly, hardworking professionals. Most casting directors have a passion for this business and are knowledgeable about it, experienced in it and very good at what they do.

Unfortunately, the nature of this business is, much of the time, filled with production deadlines and casting desires that could always use a little more time to deliver on.

Most casting directors will tell you that they often just do not have the luxury of a lot of time in which to get it all done. So if they seem brisk or rushed, or if you perceive them as all business or unfriendly, you might be right. But learn not to take it personally. Usually it has nothing to do with you.

Ultimately, it is not your perception of them that matters. Rather, it is their perception of *you* that matters most.

For those of you who are new to all this, let me give you a very brief overview of the typical casting process. It generally begins when a script is completed or nearly completed. A breakdown of the script is prepared (this is a listing of all of the characters who appear in that script and some descriptive information about each role to be cast, such as individual characteristics, age, attitude, etc.). Sometime during that process, the creative team begins conversations with the casting director about who they would like to meet with, audition or offer parts to for the lead roles. They also turn to the casting director for his or her thoughts or suggestions for the guest stars and other roles to be filled.

The casting director often comes away from these meetings facing a huge task—and while technology has changed the way most of them do business, it has not necessarily made it an easier or simpler process.

The tools are different, but in the new business of acting, some methods and procedures that are rooted in the past remain a constant today. The technology has sped up the process and the playing field may have leveled a bit (now that actors have the ability to and are requested on many occasions to self-submit on certain roles in certain projects), the casting process still exists within a business in which there are more applicants seeking the relatively few jobs available than there are jobs to fill.

Auditions are job interviews—and when the day arrives (and it is coming) that all of your job interviews are a completely virtual (as opposed to in-person) experience, the stakes will become even higher. It will be much easier for a casting director to simply delete your digital audition after watching it for just a few seconds than it is for him to take the time to meet with you in person and sit through a potentially bad audition or to have to devote the time to an actor whose audition in the first few seconds indicates that he or she is not right for the role.

How you "present" is beyond critical. To approach it any other way will weaken your career potential.

Auditions are also one more very significant component of both an action plan and a career. They are, if handled professionally, strategically and smartly, important opportunities for you to market yourself as a both a person and a brand.

One of the mistakes that many actors make is that they focus too much energy (or all of their energy) in preparing for an audition to get a single job, when, actually, their focus instead belongs on both preparing for the best audition they are capable of *and* being cognizant of the bigger picture of their career in the process.

From *The Business of Acting* perspective, the goal of any audition is *not* first and foremost to get cast in the role, but to, instead, cast a favorable impression on the casting director. It was true in the old business of acting and it remains true in the new business of acting. Careers are not built on single jobs. They are constructed from years of hard work, ongoing training and, perhaps most importantly, relationships.

Let's break down the various pieces.

A lot has to happen before an audition comes your way. Then you will have to be lucky enough to be selected from among the hundreds, if not thousands, of submissions a casting director receives (whether you self-submitted or your agent or manager made the submission). The odds are that you, like most of your fellow actors, are not getting the opportunity to audition as often as you think you should.

This often triggers a predictable, but unfortunate, behavior pattern. You quickly become too invested in the outcome of this particular audition (an acting job), instead of realizing that, going in, even though you beat the odds against yourself by being called in at all, you still have another huge hurdle to overcome: the sizeable odds against you actually getting the role you audition for.

Don't get me wrong. Of course I want you to get it—and I want you to be so confident and prepared for this opportunity that you deserve the job. But deserving it in the business of acting is not enough. In the business of talent casting, it is not the *best* actor who gets the job; it is the *right* actor who gets hired.

It would be nice (and even fair) if the best actor and the right actor were the same person, but among the pool of working actors, that is not, unfortunately, an easy combination to come by.

So if getting the job is not the win, what is? It is the opportunity to meet (perhaps for the first time or to get reintroduced to) a casting director whose career, like yours, is not rooted in the role they are auditioning you for, but in lots of roles and lots of projects both today and in the future.

Turn every audition situation into a big win by giving a great audition and, in the process, making a great impression so that that casting director will be more likely to bring you in for other roles on the series they work on or other projects they will later become involved with. Be memorable for all of the right reasons.

With every step, there are lessons to be learned. Here is one . . .

Each semester in The Business of Acting class, I invite a panel of recent former students to return to class to talk with my current students about their transitions from college to the real world. I ask them to talk about the early, professional situations they have found themselves in since graduating, how prepared they felt for the situations they were in and what they learned about themselves as people, as actors, as businesses and as brands in the process.

One of my favorite former students came to class with a particularly significant story about a recent audition.

Mike, who early on learned how to be a very proactive actor, found himself being called in to audition for a role in an independent film. He walked into the reception area at the casting director's office to find nearly a dozen very well built, very studly-attractive, very tall actors in his age range waiting to audition for the same role. Get the picture? I should disclose at this point that Mike is not any of those things, physically.

Mike told of how his immediate internal response after scanning the waiting room was, "What the #@!* am I doing here?" He double-checked with the casting assistant to confirm that the role he was called in for was actually the role they wanted to see him for and, indeed, it was.

A bit baffled, but undaunted, Mike took a seat and tried to concentrate on his fast-approaching audition, trying hard not to pay attention to the rising levels of testosterone around him. Clearly, the casting director knew what Mike looked like when he selected him to audition; all of his vital information is clearly printed on his resume. He tried not to think about that.

One by one, the hunks who arrived before him were called in. Then, it was his turn. Mike entered the casting director's office and, his confidence holding him steady and being very much prepared, he did his audition and left.

It was a few days later that Mike, who had by this time put that particular audition experience completely out of his mind, got the call that he had booked the role.

How could that possibly have happened? The casting director auditioned nearly 30 male model types and one Mike—and Mike booked the job.

Once on the set, Mike, very happy about landing the job, but nonetheless still curious about how the role came to him, started asking questions.

He learned that while the film's director wanted what my friend, headshot and production photographer and cinematographer Michael Lamont, calls "heavy breathing," the smart and savvy casting director, who, of course, also read the script, thought there was room within the role to toss a "red herring" into the casting process, something unexpected to throw the director (and possibly an audience) off the trail.

After an afternoon of "heavy breathing" types, Mike walked in to audition. The director, who was present at the initial casting session, saw Mike as almost a breath of fresh air.

It turned out that the casting director's "red herring" was a calculated risk that paid off across the board. The casting director proved to be a creative hero, the director got to reinvent what was to be a rather inconsequential role and Mike got and earned a valuable new credit on his resume early in his career journey.

The lesson here: never allow yourself to be influenced by what you see when you walk into the waiting room. You never know.

That was Mike's story. But it could have gone a very different way if Mike was a different kind of person and a less empowered actor. This is where behavior, the wrong kind of behavior, can hurt you. When I went undercover as an actor, I was astonished by some of the behavior I witnessed in casting office waiting rooms.

Here is what you may not know: what happens in the reception area while you wait for your turn to audition matters, a lot. The casting director may be behind closed doors with another actor, but odds are she has an associate, an assistant or an intern who is paying very close attention to what transpires while the other actors are waiting to be seen.

An actor who goes to any audition feeling anything less than one hundred percent confident and prepared is setting himself up for the evil energy that can circulate among eager, overeager or desperate actors in an audition waiting room.

Usually, auditions happen by categories. All of the actors who are up for the same role you are up for are usually scheduled to audition in the same block of time, meaning that when you arrive at the casting director's office, it is more than likely that you will come face to face with many of the other actors who are up for the same role that you are up for. Ignore them!

The empowered actor simply signs in for his audition and quietly waits for his turn. The desperate actor will quickly become threatened by every other actor in the room, thinking such destructive thoughts as, "He looks more like the guy they're looking for than I do," or "I just saw him on a big commercial; he's bound to get this, too," or "Everyone here seems to know him; that can't be good for me."

Never let this happen to you. Never.

Your perception of what you might observe in these situations is far from accurate. Your focus, instead, needs to be on why you are there, not on who you perceive the competition to be.

For the actor who is easily emotionally influenced by this situation, these feelings will alter your behavior. Never allow room for anything less than a professional, positive attitude in these situations. At the same time, anything you do that appears to distract or throw another actor off his mark in his preparation to go into the room when it is his turn at bat will get reported back to the casting director later.

I hear this time and time again from casting directors. No matter how well an actor does in the audition, if the casting director hears that the actor was disrespectful to anyone in their office, including other actors waiting to audition, they will not call that actor back for fear that, should he be lucky enough to actually go on to book the job, there might be, would be or could be behavioral issues with this person on set.

Another important factor in the audition process from the casting director's perspective is what I call "The First Two Seconds Test."

Before you have uttered a word of your audition material, the casting director will have already formed an opinion about whether or not you are the right actor for the job from the energy and the attitude you bring with you into the room in the first two seconds when you walk into your audition—or the first two seconds of watching your virtual audition video.

During my stint as an undercover actor, one of the auditions I was sent out on was for a small role in a one-hour network drama. It was one of those to-remain-unnamed-for-reasons-that-will-soon-be-apparent lawyer shows.

I arrived at the audition fully prepared to do the best job I could both as an actor and as an observer of the audition process. With every audition I was lucky enough to be called in for, I always paid keen attention to everything that was happening around me. While I kept one eye on my sides in preparation for the inevitable, I had the other eye on every other (real) actor in the waiting room. Was there any conversation going on? If so, what was being said? What was the energy in the room? It was all so fascinating to observe—and to be immersed in.

When it became my turn to enter the casting director's office, he greeted me from behind his desk, instructed me to have a seat in front of him, asked if I had any questions (I did not), then proceeded to read the scene with me.

When we were done, he paused for few seconds and said, "That was very good." I was cringing on the inside. It was not supposed to be "good," it was just supposed to "be."

He then asked me if I would try it again and gave me a few notes to consider in tweaking my next attempt. It began anew.

When we had finished the second stab at the sides, the casting director, looking rather pleasant and friendly, paused for a few more seconds and then said, "That was really good. We are having callbacks for the producers in an hour. I would like you to stick around."

"Stick around?!" I was thinking to myself, "Was he kidding? Really?!"

Indeed, it was no joke. I was being brought to a callback with the producers and director of this episode of the series.

"Crap!" I said to myself. "What do I do now?!"

The objective of my going undercover as an actor was for me to as objectively as possible (not really being an actor) witness first-hand and experience the *process* of going on an audition, not actually land a role.

As the casting director waited for me to acknowledge his invitation to the callback, several thoughts were racing through my mind, like, "What do I do *now*?"

As I considered the ramifications and repercussions of coming clean to him about who I was and why I was there, I could imagine him having me thrown off the lot by studio security and vowing never to audition or hire any of my clients, ever.

But that never happened.

Calmly, but somewhat nervously, I explained to him who I really was and that my purpose being there was not to really get cast in any role, but to be able to write and teach real actors what they need to know to ace the process, make a great impression and hopefully, eventually, get hired.

I went on and on for what felt like ten minutes. In actuality, I'm sure it was just seconds. But, when your professional and personal ass is on the line, the passage of time tends to feel a little skewed.

I soon finished my rant of an explanation. For me, it was clearly rooted in "Please don't hit me, please don't yell at me, please don't hold my clients responsible."

After I got my last word out, without skipping a beat, the casting director, who never took his eye off of me, looked me straight in the eye and said, "Does that mean you're not going to the callback?"

I was speechless. Really?

There is a big lesson here. For me, this was perhaps the biggest reveal of my entire undercover actor experience.

The casting director did not care if I was Brad Lemack the manager or Brad Lemack the undercover actor. The only thing he cared about was that he believed that I was one of the few right candidates from among all the actors he auditioned for this role. It was his job to deliver to the producers four actors for them to consider, who could all play the role—and he did his job.

You may be wondering if I actually followed through and went on the callback. I did. Remember, this was a research project!

Luckily for me, I did not book the role. But something else rather interesting happened. During the next season, this casting director called me in directly for three other producers' sessions for three other roles that had come up in the same series. Each time his office would call me, I reminded his assistant who I was and that I was not an actor. It never mattered.

I aced "The First Two Seconds Test" my first time at bat and that was enough. Each of the roles they called me in for were roles the casting director believed I was right for and should be considered for.

Again, luck was on my side. While I did go in when called, I never booked any of the roles, but I did come away from each audition with a deeper and deeper appreciation and respect for those of you who really do this (and are on the way to doing this) for a living and for a career.

My point—and I admit I took the long road to get here—is that the casting director's perception of you, albeit subjective, is a critical component in this process.

Too many actors try too hard to make a good first impression and end up, instead, making fools of themselves. The casting director does not really care about the kind of day you are having or how tough it was for you to find a place to park.

They are not mean or unkind people (most of them); they just have a job to do. They want you to come in, be great, be professional and get out.

How you approach an audition and how you behave throughout your time there, while important components on this part of your journey, are trumped by how you process the experience once it is over.

The goal is to never leave an audition feeling that, if you had an opportunity to do it again, you would do anything different. Allowing room in your brain for this thought will only stir negativity about the experience and a drop in self-confidence if/when you do not get the part, which is why getting the part should never be the primary goal.

If you gave a prepared, professional audition and if you were personally appropriate and pleasant in the process, then it should be looked at as nothing but a win-win for your career.

Since talent has little, if anything, to do with who gets the job, and since it is the right actor, not the best actor, who gets the job, the win for you is a positive connection with a casting person that will serve you throughout your career. The win for the casting director is that she now knows one new (to her) actor, who is invested in their career, whom she knows she can and will count on in a future audition situation.

CHAPTER 6

SELF-SUBMITTING:

The Art of Selectivity in Pursuing Casting Opportunities

THERE HAS NEVER been a better time to be an unrepresented actor. It has also become the landscape in which there is no excuse for any lack of proactivity in the pursuit of a career, whether you are represented or not.

When my first book was published, actors did not have the luxury, the availability or the general opportunity to legitimately submit themselves for very many professional television and film acting roles, unless they were stealing or otherwise getting their hands on the hard copy Breakdowns that were the tools of—and in the domain solely of—agents, managers and casting directors. This, of course, is separate from the theatre casting opportunities that regularly appeared in publications such as *Back Stage*.

Since that time, while the playing field may not have leveled completely, it has definitely tilted more than a little bit in favor of the proactive actor. However, with opportunity comes responsibility and restraint—and here is where the potential problem with access to this information begins.

The Internet has made available a plethora of information and resources for all of us. Perhaps too much.

Recently I Googled a variety of words and terms related to actors, auditions, casting services, casting breakdowns and acting career services and literally thousands of listings were generated. How could anyone possibly sort through all of this information, evaluate each service listed and make a determination as to which one or ones to use or to avoid? The short answer is to ask about and to listen to the experiences of fellow actors who have made the mistakes before that you want to avoid making now.

In my Business of Acting class at the Emerson College Los Angeles Center, the midterm assignment my students are asked to complete involves them becoming Internet detectives. They are each asked to use the Internet to conduct some broad research and then select four websites that claim to offer career-enhancing services for actors. They use search terms similar to the ones I mentioned earlier.

The assignment asks that they dig around and once they have selected the sites they want to focus on, they are asked to assess, evaluate and analyze both the credibility and the value of the online services offered.

Back in the classroom, when the students present their findings, they take us directly to the websites they selected and give us a tour of what they discovered. As a part of their presentation, they relate what their findings are and why they came to the conclusions they arrived at. By the end of the class, depending on the number of students enrolled that semester, we all come away with anywhere from 40 to 50 websites and online services that any actor should avoid at any cost.

The smart, empowered, proactive actor must learn how to spot a fraud, a scam or a fake service that is out to take your money and does nothing more than display your photo and resume for the world to see on a site that no industry person ever uses or is even aware of.

As long as the Internet remains unregulated in this sense, you must proceed with caution when signing up for any online service, whether it is a pay-for-service site or not. Remember, there is a value in capturing your personal information that any website can use and/or sell to any other website (or other business) for its own gain and profit. You have a personal obligation and a professional responsibility to perform due diligence in any business transaction you enter into, particularly online.

Having now thrown out all of the warnings, let's look at how to know "legit" when you see it—and where to find it. While there are plenty of websites to stay away from, there are many that offer services that do actually deliver value and opportunity, if used smartly and strategically.

We have a short list of reliable Web resources for actors on the Resources page at TheBusinessOfActing.com. To make that list, a site has to have proven itself a true industry resource that is actually used by legitimate industry professionals.

As of this writing, the primary go-to sources include the long-established Breakdown Services and the later-established entry into the field, Casting Networks.

Gary Marsh established Breakdown Services, Ltd., in 1971 as a service to agents and managers that fulfilled their needs to submit their clients for auditions with the needs of casting directors who were seeking actors to audition. In a five-part interview I did with Gary for our Web TV series *Inside the Business of Acting* (InsideTheBusi nessOfActing.com), he talks about the early roots of his business and how, as the landscape has changed, so, too, have the services that his company offers to the industry. It is well worth watching to get a complete picture of the transformation that has occurred at Breakdown Services, now a global company, and how this trans formation has created opportunities for actors that were never available before to them. Indeed, Marsh is an industry pioneer.

Once, not too long ago, a packet from Breakdown Services would arrive very early in the morning at talent representatives' offices all around Los Angeles and New York. The hard copy delivery contained breakdowns on every television, film, theatre and other related project being cast at the moment. Each hard copy page broke down each of these projects into the roles being cast, the storyline of the project and all relevant information pertaining to the project (dates it would shoot, where it would shoot, producer/ director names, etc.). Each morning, we who represent talent would diligently, carefully, review every entry in the packet and from that review determine who among our clients we would sub mit for audition consideration.

This information was never available to actors. It also was not available to just anyone who called themselves an agent or man ager. Then, like today, if you wanted to subscribe to this service, before you were accepted to pay for it, you would have to qualify to receive it. This was and remains an important factor in the self submission discussion. It was designed to ensure that only those people who were legitimate agents or managers could get confiden tial casting information that casting directors did not want to get into the hands of actors.

Talent representatives are expected to use their professional expertise in evaluating casting breakdowns and in selecting who among their clients, if anyone, is completely appropriate for submitting on any given role. Casting directors count on agents and managers to have the professional objectivity in making these decisions that actors themselves cannot easily make when given the same information about audition opportunities, which is why casting breakdowns were never intended to be seen by actors, only by the people who represent them.

We have come a long way in a short period of time from the days of hard copy submissions. As the technology created the opportunity for Breakdown Services to deliver their content online, the opportunity for actors to purchase or otherwise get their hands on this information was ramped up several notches, if it was possible at all.

It was not terribly unusual not so long ago that an underpaid agent's or manager's assistant would simply copy the hard copy breakdowns that came in every day and sell the copyright-protected materials illegally to any actor who was willing to pay for it. Let's not throw the spotlight on this criminal activity to just the occasional assistant; there were also the cases of greedy agents and managers who themselves would sell the materials to their own clients and to other actors.

This activity resulted in two significant things: casting directors who had become used to the hundreds, if not thousands, of submissions they would receive from talent representatives for every role they were casting were then also getting hundreds, if not thousands, more envelopes to open with submissions to review that they did not want from actors. This had a negative effect across the entire casting/submission process.

Given the time limitations given to a casting director to cast a single role and/or an entire project, many would instead, often (or routinely), call or otherwise do business with only the talent representatives they had established relationships with. Actors represented by other agents and/or managers all paid the price for that decision because the opportunity to submit clients for a role would be eliminated easily, simply because of the volume of submissions casting directors were having to deal with—or choosing not to.

In the meantime, actors who were paying to get unauthorized access to this information were then reviewing the contents with the subjective eye toward getting their money's worth on their investment and were more inclined to submit on roles they really were not appropriate for, further cluttering the casting director's in-box.

There was a general tendency among many actors to simply ignore whether a role was classified as a lead or as a co-star. Regardless of their level of experience (or inexperience) and what credits they had earned (or not), if a role seemed to fit them in terms of age, physical attributes or other quality, the actor would just submit himself for it. This was in no one's best interest, least of all, the actor who made the submission.

In the new business of acting, most casting submissions made by agents and managers are done electronically, much to the joy of most casting directors whose offices are no longer flooded with piles of envelopes waiting to be opened and other piles of submissions often ignored due to the sheer volume of mail and submissions that needed to be processed with the release of each breakdown.

The transformation of the professional submission business to an online platform has also, thankfully, made it much more difficult for actors to steal, purchase or otherwise get their hands on this content. Those who did soon learned that because electronic breakdowns are embedded with certain codes and all codes connect to a specific account, all submissions are now traceable.

It was not an unusual practice for Breakdown Services to occasionally issue a blind, bogus breakdown for a blind, bogus project just to see who was submitting on it, providing a perfect opportunity in the process to catch a thief. Entrapment? Hardly. Effective? Enormously.

So while the business and trade of illegal breakdowns plummeted, a new, legal opportunity developed for both the information providers and for actors seeking access to casting opportunities.

The question arose out of the recognition that there was, indeed, a legitimate market for this information. In the new business of acting, many in the casting community were discovering that there was a need (albeit with discretion) to reach out directly to actors, not in any attempt to bypass talent representatives, but rather to locate talent for smaller, very specific roles that some agents and managers would often not bother to submit on. Then there was the huge pool of nonunion and/or unrepresented actors who were rarely in the loop, but nonetheless represented a sizeable community amongst themselves.

In a new landscape that has generated a massive amount of new roles to cast (particularly for typically low-paying new media and nonunion projects), casting directors needed some kind of filter system to cast their nets as broadly as possible to see who else was out there. But the question quickly became: How do you serve these needs without compromising the quality and integrity of the submissions you would receive?

At the end of the day, the casting director is charged with filling a role with the right actor. How that actor comes to them is becoming less critical than finding him or her in the first place.

This change in attitude, landscape and technology quickly gave birth to several legitimate online submission services to specifically bring casting opportunities to actors and the opportunity for casting directors to become acquainted with new or less-often-seen (or submitted) talent.

The first service out of the gate came, not surprisingly, right from the offices of Breakdown Services. Gary Marsh saw an opportunity to both bridge the gaps that existed in this process and to serve the entire community.

Launching Actors Access (at ActorsAccess.com) gave casting directors who were already using the Breakdown Services system the added opportunity to release certain breakdowns of roles in certain projects directly to actors, affording actors in the system the opportunity to be their own agent or manager in evaluating the role, deciding if they are right for it, then submitting on it or not. Often, a role that appears on Actors Access has not been released to agents and managers, depending on the kind of role or type of project it is.

The same is true for the casting service Casting Networks (Cast ingNetworks.com)—which, at this writing, operates L.A. Casting, N.Y. Casting and San Francisco Casting—which has grown to service primarily the commercial industry and the talent representatives and casting directors who work in this area.

The self-submission piece of L.A. Casting (and their related entities) works much in the same way that the Actors Access service functions and is typically heavy with nonunion and non-paying student film projects, but these all still represent potentially important opportunities to build your resume, particularly in the early stages of your career.

Other online self-submission services for actors currently exist, including the relatively recent (as of this writing) entry into the field The Casting Frontier (TheCastingFrontier.com).

Others will have come and gone as this book endures, but the viable, valuable services that are actually used and respected by industry professionals will remain.

All of these services will charge you a fee for usage. Some will let you sign up for free and even let you upload your photo and resume for free; others will charge you for this. Some will allow you to self-submit for a per-submission fee; others will offer you a package of unlimited submissions for a fixed, yearly charge. All will afford you the opportunity to upload video clips and demos, usually for an additional fee, to be included in the online profile you create for yourself. All of these materials are then available for you to select from and to use at your discretion in the self-submissions you choose to make.

The accounts you create for yourself on Actors Access, Casting Networks and The Casting Frontier are also accessed by your agent and/or manager in submissions they make on your behalf. Your Actors Access account gets linked to your representative's (Breakdown Services) account; the same with your Casting Networks and Casting Frontier accounts.

When making submissions, the online resume you create is attached to the submission made for you. The photo selected by your agent or manager to front the submission is chosen from among the photos you have uploaded to these services.

Indeed, it is a business partnership where all parties must perform due diligence for the system to work as designed and as intended.

What kinds of roles will you find available for you to self-submit on? Clearly, actors will not find lead roles in network pilots on self-submission services, but you can find supplemental and support opportunities that are worth exploring. Services like Actors Access have also become clearinghouses for roles in student films, nonunion projects, Web series and other new media endeavors, not to mention theatre and other live projects.

For the unrepresented actor, these legitimate, professional services, if used correctly, can allow to you be proactive in the process of launching your action plan and moving forward on your career journey in ways never before available to actors.

Information can be powerful, but, in the wrong hands, it can be harmful. How you use the information you are allowed legal access to is critical. In the same way actors not very long ago were shooting themselves in the feet by not being smart about the self-submissions they made through illegally obtained breakdowns, it is critical today to use your legal access strategically and wisely. Do not submit on a role unless you are *absolutely* right for it.

The danger you potentially create for yourself by not following these guidelines is the emotional letdown of knowing that you have submitted for a certain number of roles and have not gotten an audition for any of them.

Your submit-to-audition ratio is going to vary, depending on lots of factors; most are intangible. But what will remain a reality and a constant is the need for you to decrease your odds of being overlooked by making only appropriate submissions.

It is a numbers game on both sides. Actors tend to think that the more frequently they self-submit, they more frequently they will get an audition. At the same time, casting directors on any project have a limited amount of time to cast the role and a limited amount of time to audition a limited number of actors.

Given that the number of submissions they receive for any role they are casting is tremendous (whether the breakdown goes out to just talent representatives, just actors or both), there is very little time for a casting director to look at the sea of thumbnail head shots on their computer screens and, from that, select the relatively few lucky souls who will get the opportunity to audition for them. In Chapter 3, "The Art of the Head Shot," we addressed how to make your thumbnail photo pop out in this sea of images. Now, let's look at the numbers.

The odds of generating an audition from a self-submission are against you; those odds are also against agents and managers who submit on a client's behalf. So, knowing that going in, how do you increase your odds?

Always make sensible submissions. If you represent yourself as an agent or manager would, you can feel confident that your self-submission was not overlooked, skipped over or otherwise dismissed for any reason other than the numbers.

If a casting director only has slots for 15 actors and you were 16th on their choice list, there is nothing you can do about it—and you will never know. You either get the opportunity to audition or it goes to someone else. That's business. With another self-submission on another project for another role, it will be your turn.

As the casting industry's further use of the technology currently available (and still to be developed) evolves, one day soon, most, if not all, auditions will be done virtually. Some self-submission services, like Breakdown Services, have already incorporated this feature and this opportunity for casting directors to use, should they choose, on some or all of their projects, for some or all of the roles they have to cast.

Soon this will become the norm, which will speed up the audition process, but which will also, unfortunately, take away the opportunity for actors and casting directors to actually meet face to face and the ability to make a personal connection. When this happens, you will be completely judged by the audition you give, not by the person you are or the energy you bring with you when you walk into the room. This is too bad. "The First Two Seconds Test" will then become "The First Micro-Second Test."

While the role might be cast quicker (and with less cost incurred by both actor and casting director—you will save the transportation costs of getting to and from the audition; the casting director will save dollars by eliminating the need for assistants and other costs that have been normal expenses for running these sessions), as voice mail and e-mail now often keep us from making personal and business connections and the opportunity to develop both personal and business relationships, virtual auditions will, unfortunately, keep actors and most casting directors an additional step removed from each other.

What if you have an agent or manager? Should you still self-submit? I frequently have this conversation with my clients, my students, actors I meet at workshops and through inquiries I receive through my Business of Acting Blog. The short answer is yes.

Eventually, there will come a point on your journey that it does not make sense for you to continue to self-submit. You will know that time has arrived when it is time to grow your resume beyond the kind of, and the level of, opportunities available to you through the self-submission services.

At that point, leave the submitting to those who represent you and begin a new level of proactivity in support of this new phase of your career journey.

Until you get there, the opportunity in the new business of acting to actually be meaningfully able to launch and build your career has never been easier—or more effective for the smart, empowered and strategic actor.

CHAPTER 7

UNIONS AND ACTORS

I N THE CATEGORY of most-asked questions in my college classes, in my workshops and seminars and through my Business of Acting Blog, fall inquiries regarding the actor unions, not so much about Actors Equity Association (AEA), but more about AFTRA (American Federation of Television and Radio Artists) and, mostly, about SAG (Screen Actors Guild).

The new business of acting is full of changes in the landscape across the board, but the area of greatest flux (as of this writing) and the area in need of some serious reinventing is the unions.

I have nothing against them, on the surface, for the protection and standards they have been created to provide their members, but it is behind the scenes where some serious attention needs to be paid if the unions are to continue to be in and of service to its current members and to those who strive to become members at the right time on their career journeys.

Another one of the biggest mistakes young actors (or new-to-the-business actors at any age) make is in rushing to join one of the actor unions. The drive, the focus, the motivation to achieve this goal too soon can be distracting and counterproductive to the goal of any action plan, which is to launch your journey, build your resume and grow a working, professional career.

Both SAG and AFTRA are currently in a healing, make-nice, stage, after having come through a very public, very image-bruising and very member-divisive contract battle in 2009. As of this writing, things are fairly calm and quiet on the union front. From where I sit, the biggest losers in that battle were the unions themselves who suffered from public displays of nasty behavior on both sides that did not serve either of the entities or their members well.

Let's look at what got us to that point, for a bit of perspective in terms of what it means for actors going forward from here.

It is all about economics. Traditionally, television and radio (as in projects that were shot or recorded on video tape or audio tape) were the domain of AFTRA; film (as in projects that were shot on film) was the domain of SAG. For the most part, throughout their histories, both unions co-existed fairly well. Because most professional actors worked in all mediums, most (but not all) actors were members of both unions; many were also members of Actors Equity, whose jurisdiction has been and is theatre.

For this discussion, we will concentrate on AFTRA and SAG.

Both unions operate as separate businesses. Although sharing many members, each has its separate administrative staff, board of directors and president. Each also has its own separate qualifications to join, as well as the financial obligations and requirements that come with union membership.

Over the years, given that the jurisdiction of each of these two unions was also so separate and unique, there has been some interest in, talk about and attempts to merge both entities into one union that would serve all actors who work in television, radio and film, regardless of the medium that captured their work (film or tape).

When my first book came out in 2002, there was a rather active movement at the time for a merger to take place and many thought that day was near. But it did not happen.

What did happen shortly thereafter was a shift in the landscape that began the early stages of the new business of acting.

Since that time, there has been an explosion of project development, production work and jobs for actors and others in new media, ranging from Web series to Internet-only commercial campaigns to interactive platforms for the at-home entertainment market.

At the same time, the industry saw massive growth (followed less than a decade later by significant decline) in consumers' interest in entertainment on, first, home video, then DVD, that they could rent or purchase for viewing on demand. Suddenly there was a marketplace for content previously, generally, thought of as having little use.

Studios quickly realized the tremendous value in product that was locked up in vaults that could become be a huge boon to their bottom lines. And it was.

Old television series that were once big hits, other television series that served niche demographics, specific genre films and products in many other categories quickly caught the eyes and the wallets of fans globally who in short time developed ferocious appetites for home entertainment they could call their own.

Old content was being repurposed and new content that was being produced for straight-to-video/DVD release was proving to be a gold mine for everyone involved, except the actors who appeared in these projects—and that is where much of the 2009 contract wars were rooted.

Years earlier, when television shows were produced during the early days of live television through the 1960s, it seemed that no one ever thought there would be any interest in or a market for repeating these programs. As the U.S. domestic syndication business began and flourished (and as interest in and demand for U.S.-produced content grew in Europe and other international television markets), old shows like *I Love Lucy, Gilligan's Island, The Brady Bunch* and countless others were sold market by market, or station by station, creating a revenue stream for the owners of these products, but not for the actors who brought the shows to life through the roles they inhabited.

Residuals for actors, meaning pay for reuse of your work, grew out of this era. It may have been too late for the actors of those old shows (or their families or estates) to reap the benefits of the new residual rules, but they did pave the way for contemporary working actors to build their bank accounts (or, in many cases, just survive) from their union-negotiated earnings from previous work when those projects were sold into broadcast or cable syndication, or later for home entertainment video, then DVD/Blu-ray.

Whereas there was little, if no, insight in the 1950s of what would later become a burgeoning market for reruns, there was also very little prognostication about the dollars that stood to be (and were later) generated from video and DVD sales.

Union contract negotiators were not immune to this inability to foresee the future, so new contracts that were negotiated with the studios and with the producers were done so in good faith, with due diligence having been performed at the time, in seeking and securing what then appeared fair compensation for reuse of actors' work in these then-new platforms.

During the home video and DVD sales explosion in the 1990s, indeed, studios and producers were making money from products they thought basically were of little or no practical value, while the actors whose work they were profiting from continued to see very little from this success.

I watched as my many of my own clients who had appeared as series regulars in hit shows that became popular again in home entertainment became more and more frustrated over a growing double-edged sword. They and their shows were being rediscovered and a fresh popularity was emerging, but every time a fan would write the series star about how much they were enjoying owning their own copies of the actors' shows, the actors could not help but wonder why they were not getting a bigger piece the pie.

At the same time, cable networks, like TV Land, were arriving on the scene embracing both the actors and their former hit series as they were attracting and building their own new (cable) audiences. It was great exposure for the actors and a big hit with TV (comedy) fans, but again the actors in these shows were learning how little the union's contract for cable use (or reuse) was worth to them.

It is hard to feel fiscally fit and financially sound when you see that lots of people (and companies) are making big bucks off your work, except you.

The unions, particularly SAG, since most of the work in question was produced on film under SAG contracts, were becoming increasingly aware of this frustrating situation that was impacting so many of their members.

This gets us back to the "it is all rooted in economics" discussion.

Since union members pay dues to their union based on a calculation that is rooted in a percentage of what the member earns during each reporting period, it became in the unions' financial interest to pursue a change to the status quo that would benefit both parties. Actors would see more pay from old work and the unions would benefit by getting a larger chunk of dues money into its coffers resulting from members earning higher pay for performance reuse.

This pay-based-on-what-you-earn structure is also at the root of the animosity that grew and the battle that erupted between AFTRA and SAG leaders (and many of their respective and mutual members) during the contract negotiation and voting in 2009. It is also rooted in the shift in the production and delivery mechanism landscape that has been sparked by the need for, and production of, content for new media platforms.

The burning question was, and perhaps, arguably, remains, what is the medium of digitally-produced content? It is not film; it is not tape. How then, for union jurisdiction purposes, do you classify it and how then do you determine in whose domain, in whose control, it falls into?

Good luck with that one.

Both AFTRA and SAG began laying claim to projects and productions that are captured digitally and both unions have now developed their own New Media contracts to deal with the new landscape. The bigger picture of what this shift has created has meant that SAG and AFTRA, whose jurisdiction for years was so clearly defined, are now pitted each against the other in the race to acquire digital projects and producers, one by one, to their side, each claiming to offer the better entity and service with which to be associated.

Whichever union sanctions a project is the union to whom actor members must pay their dues, based on the actor's total income for the reporting period for that union. If it is a SAG project, those credits go into the SAG column; if it is an AFTRA-sanctioned project, it is the AFTRA bank account that you contribute to. If it is a nonunion project—and now many are (with the scorn of both unions directed toward them), then no dues are owed to any entity.

Many television productions that had been SAG-contracted projects also began switching sides during the 2009 round of negotiations. This resulted in AFTRA claiming more productions as their own, as well as claiming and receiving dues from their members from work in these now AFTRA projects, dollars that formerly went to SAG.

Of course the dollars you might earn in a nonunion project could be considerably less than a union-sanctioned production, but in this landscape, with the many, many low-budget union projects being produced, that is not always the case. More about nonunion work options and the implications and benefits of these opportunities later.

An unfortunate change in the landscape that neither actor nor union, studio or producer is benefiting from is the tremendous amount of revenue lost to all parties from the skyrocketing problem of piracy.

You deserve to get paid for your work The enormous sums lost to piracy not only cost the unions dues income from the money performers never see, but, more importantly, from the artists' perspective, this is lost revenue that can have a significant impact on their bottom lines.

Let's look at the nuts and bolts of what it takes—and what it means to be a union member in the new business of acting.

In order to join SAG, you must first find yourself a job that requires SAG membership of you or you must earn and collect (as of this writing) three vouchers from nonunion extra work in a SAG-sanctioned project. Each day of extra work can generate one voucher, if they are made available. However, not all SAG productions will make them available to all non-SAG extras—and there have been discussions over the years about upping the number of required vouchers to make SAG membership more difficult to obtain.

Earning the designated number of vouchers will also earn you SAG-Eligible status, meaning that the door is then open for you to join the Guild.

Many nonunion actors earn SAG-Eligible status by getting hired through a classification well known and often used in the business of acting called Taft-Hartley.

Back in 1947, Senator Robert Taft (R, Ohio) and Representative Fred A. Hartley, Jr. (R, New Jersey) sponsored legislation that had nothing to do with the entertainment industry at the time, but has since become a much-used verb in the industry. To be "Taft-Hartley'd" means that a nonunion actor can be hired to fill a union job if there is no union worker to fill the role. It worked—and still does for any industry in which a union plays a large (controlling) influence. In fact, the original goal of the law was to monitor the activities and power of labor unions.

Today it has taken on special meaning in the business of acting. Being so designated by a casting director and/or production company allows an actor to play a union role and opens the doors to full union membership in the process.

As easy as it sounds, there are still hoops that have to be jumped through to make this happen. The designation has to first be justified to the union. "Why hire this nonunion actor over any one of the many union actors who are available to work?" is the essence of the argument that needs to be made to give a union job to a nonunion actor—and this is where your special skills and the unique abilities that you alone bring to a role can make the case sway in your favor.

The commercial casting business is a frequent applier of the Taft-Hartley provision because, often, it is, indeed, something unique about one actor over another that makes him or her the right actor for a commercial role. Many nonunion actors gain entry to SAG through this means of designation.

Being "Taft-Hartley'd" does not mean that you must pay up and join the union immediately, which holds its own financial appeal to often cash-strapped actors. Detailed information about the process is available at SAG.org. You will also find direct links on the Resources page at TheBusinessOfActing.com.

The other currently available way into SAG membership is employment in a project under an affiliate union's (AFTRA, AGMA, AEA, ACTRA) contract in nothing less than a principal role.

Getting the work itself is not enough, however. While you may have earned the qualifications to join SAG, you still have to have the funds available to you to pay the costs of membership.

As of this writing, initiation dues for SAG membership are

$2,277. There are minimum dues that you are required to pay each year, regardless of whether or not you have worked in a SAG-sanctioned job. Minimum annual dues, as of this writing, are $116. When you first join, you are required to pay both the initiation fee and your first semi-annual dues payment of $58, for a grand total of $2,335 that must accompany your SAG membership application.

Of course, these fees and dues are tax-deductible, as allowed by law. But it can be a painful check to write nonetheless for many actors who will have earned this money the hard way, from non-acting jobs.

As a point of comparison, when my first book was published in 2002, the initiation fee to join SAG was $1,310 and the minimum annual dues were $100. That is a sizeable increase in the initiation fee for many actors whose pay received for acting work has not, in most cases, kept up with the increases in buying in to become or remaining a SAG member.

While the terms of how a nonunion actor can get his or her hands on SAG vouchers to apply for union membership may not have changed (yet), the increase in dollars needed to join has made it difficult for many actors who are in a position to join to be able to afford to do so. It is another dilemma created for the actor in transition.

Joining AFTRA is easier, at least it is as of this writing.

With the completion of an application and a check for the initiation fee, almost anyone can join AFTRA. Membership does not have to be so much as earned as it does paid for.

AFTRA's initiation fee is currently $1,600. Those members earning less than $2,000 a year from AFTRA-sanctioned projects pay minimum annual dues of $127.80. In contrast, in 2002 when

The Business of Acting was first published, AFTRA initiation fees were $1,258 and annual minimum dues were $116.

There are four other performer/artist unions that are considered affiliate unions to SAG and AFTRA to include in this discussion: Actors Equity Association (AEA), American Guild of Musical Artists (AGMA), American Guild of Variety Artists (AGVA) and Alliance of Canadian Cinema, Television and Radio Artists (ACTRA).

AEA represents actors and stage managers in the United States. There are several options for obtaining AEA membership, including employment under an Equity contract, membership in a sister union for at least one year and being a member in good standing of a parent union (if applicable). If you have worked as a performer under the union's jurisdiction on a principal or under-five contract or worked for at least three days of background work, you also become eligible to join.

As of this writing there is an initiation fee of $1,100 and basic dues of $118. The Equity Membership Candidate Program is an opportunity for actors and stage managers-in-training to credit theatrical work in an Equity theatre toward eventual membership in the Association. Visit their website at ActorsEquity.org for information.

AGMA concerns itself primarily with artists working in opera, concert, recital and ballet. Much like AFTRA, membership is a relatively simple process involving the completion of the Guild's application and the payment of an initiation fee of $500. Minimum annual dues are, as of this writing, $78. In addition, all members working under an AGMA contract have two percent of the first $100,000 gross income deducted from their paychecks classified as Working Dues.

AGVA represents performing artists and stage managers for

live performances in the variety field, including singers and dancers in touring shows and in theatrical revues, theme park performers, skaters, circus performers, comedians and stand-up comics, cabaret and club artists. Membership in AGVA is earned one of two ways, by either a contract to work in an AGVA-sanctioned project or by approval of a submitted professional resume to the Guild. As of this writing, the initiation fee is $750; minimum dues are $72 per year and increase based on a member's earnings.

ACTRA is a national Canadian organization of more than 21,000 professional performers working in the English-language recorded media. The Alliance's core mission is to protect and promote the rights of Canadian performers. As the ACTRA website informs, membership in ACTRA is open to any performer who has enrolled in their Apprentice Membership Program and has attained six professional engagements under ACTRA jurisdiction, or who has, in recognition of the barriers confronting the disabled and members of visible minorities, three professional engagements under ACTRA jurisdiction, or has membership in a sister organization (Canadian Actors Equity Association, SAG or AFTRA).

The Apprentice Membership Program is an opportunity for non-ACTRA members to begin the process of ACTRA membership. The ACTRA website, at ACTRA.com is the best place to research this organization. You will also find links to this site and, specifically, to the Alliance's Apprentice Membership Program page on the Resources page at TheBusinessOfActing.com.

The costs associated with joining ACTRA are varied. To become an Apprentice member, the initiation fee is C$75. Full membership into ACTRA through the Apprentice Program generates a second initiation fee of C$450, as well as the payment of your first year of basic dues in the amount of C$195. Full ACTRA members also pay Working Dues of 2.25 percent of their gross earnings, up to a maximum of C$4,000 per year.

Current members of the Canadian Actors Equity Association (CAEA) who wish to join ACTRA pay a reduced initiation fee of C$225 and are obligated to the same dues structure as full members.

If you are already a member of SAG, AFTRA, Equity/United Kingdom or the Media Entertainment & Arts Alliance (Australia), you can join ACTRA by paying an initiation fee of C$900, plus the C$195 annual dues. This option is triggered once you land a speaking part in an ACTRA-sanctioned project.

I never said that this was easy!

Links to all of these organizations are available on the Resources page of our website.

When to join a union, and, in many cases, if to join at all, is an important component of this discussion.

Not too long ago, a young actor client of mine had the opportunity to audition for a series regular role in a pilot for a new comedy. He impressed the casting director at his first audition and earned himself a callback. He aced the callback, as well, and we were all very excited when he was invited to a third callback with both the studio that would be producing the series and the network that would be airing it.

It was a thrilling and exhilarating adventure as he got closer and closer to getting cast in this series. As a nonunion performer up to this point, landing this job would not only elevate his profile and propel him further on his career journey, it would get him into the union.

As the casting process continued and the pool of "the chosen" was narrowed down, my client, unfortunately, was eliminated. It ended up being a choice between my guy and someone else's client and for all of those reasons that we can never quite put our finger on, the other actor booked the job (the pilot was produced, but the series was never picked up).

While my client did not book this role, he did, in the process, impress the casting director, the production company and all else involved with his talent, his good nature and his potential, which proved to pay off for him shortly thereafter.

That pilot season came and went and the casting company that was hired to cast the pilot that my client did not get was later hired to cast another comedy series that did get picked up. As that series went into production and as guest roles for the various episodes were released, we routinely submitted the client for the various roles he was appropriate for, but were unsuccessful in securing an audition for him in any of the early episodes.

One afternoon, the casting director for the series called the office to say that they had a small role in an upcoming episode that had not been released on Breakdown Services but which our client would be perfect for. In fact, he was offering the client the job without him even having to audition, with one "small" condition.

The client, who was still a nonunion actor, would need to join the union, but the company was not able to create a Taft-Hartley situation for the actor to do this role. The offer was that they would hire him if he would become a SAG member first.

It was an interesting situation. On one hand, we had the opportunity for the client to step up to the union plate and change the playing field in which he could work, if he would first invest in the opportunity and join the union. On the other hand, still in his early twenties, the actor was young enough to still benefit from the nonunion work available to him that was building both his resume and his confidence. H would be required to give up these opportunities once he joined SAG. The last consideration was that the role he was being offered would only pay him scale for the one day he would work ($782), but it would cost him $2,335 in initiation fees and dues to join the union.

What would you do?

The client and I weighed the options. His agent and I then weighed the options. Interestingly enough, it was the client's agent who argued that we should pass on this job and wait for a better opportunity.

The client and I were in agreement on the other side. We both believed that this was a valuable opportunity to seize and that given all factors and all considerations, it made sense to take the leap of faith into union membership, which we believed would more easily open the doors to other opportunities—and so the client took a partial loan from his parents, put the balance on a credit card, became a SAG member and jumped into his first union acting job.

In retrospect, was this a smart decision? For this client, yes. Having become a union member made it possible to submit him for other union work being cast by casting directors who will only see union members. While agents and managers submit nonunion clients for union projects routinely (and many of these clients will get auditions if the look is spot on and/or if their special skills trump those of a current union member), there remain casting directors of union projects who will only audition union actors.

Following this first union job, auditions for other union jobs for this client did come in, and at a rate greater than the nonunion work he had been submitted for previously—and he actually booked some important work in the wake of this decision. Like all actors, that result became cyclical.

There have been periods of much (audition) activity and many more periods of no activity, but on the whole, the investment in union membership proved to be the right one at the right time, for him. By the way, his second union job, a guest star role in an important one-hour drama, earned him enough money to pay back his parents, pay off his credit card, pay his full first year of union dues and take both his agent and me to lunch, with quite a bit left over that was saved to help cover him through the inevitable slower times ahead.

A part of this discussion about joining the union, particularly SAG or AFTRA, also needs to include a discussion about when or whether to ever get out of that relationship.

For many formerly working actors, the new business of acting has brought a significantly increased number of opportunities for nonunion work. As the amount of nonunion work has increased steadily, many union actors find themselves facing a dilemma. Once a union member, always a union member had been the mantra. It was clearly understood that once you became a union member, you were forbidden to accept work in any nonunion project under fear of, in some high profile cases, fines and/or expulsion from the union.

Not wanting to trigger a resume audit or a red flag, many union actors chose, nonetheless, to accept nonunion work, but did so under an assumed name or alias, which worked fine if the actor was truly an unknown artist. Any actor of note or of name (or face) value could not risk such an endeavor, which began to trigger the increased use of another way around this union law, a legally allowable (but not union-encouraged) option known as "Fi-Core."

Claiming Financial Core status with your union allows you to work in a nonunion project, but there is a high price to pay for taking this route, the largest being that the core of Fi-Core rests in the union member resigning from the union.

With all unions attempting to curb the growth of nonunion productions, they are clearly not encouraging their members to go this route, even if it means taking a low-paying job doing anything else over accepting a role in a nonunion project.

The complications can arise later for the Fi-Core, former union, actor who wants back into their union. It can be an uphill battle that will require you meeting the requirements of membership all over again, including the payment of whatever the going initiation fee is at the time—and that is if the union will accept you back given the circumstances of your departure.

Of course, your union would like to keep you on its membership roster. One of the reasons is that while they may want *you*, they also want your dues money—and they cannot collect dues from a resigned member. They also cannot hold you liable for dues based on income you earn from work in nonunion projects.

When to join the union should always be a personal, smart and well thought out decision based on the circumstances you are dealing with at the time.

Union membership also comes with benefits beyond ensuring the conditions under which you work and the minimums by which you are paid. Health insurance and pension plans (as well as other programs) are available to members if you qualify to receive them—but that is a big if. You have to earn a minimum amount during designated reporting periods to qualify to pay for insurance coverage of various levels. As of this writing, a SAG member needed to have been paid at least $28,120 in covered earnings during the designated period to be eligible for the union's insurance plan I or at least $13,790 or have accrued at least 74 days on SAG contract employment to be eligible to pay for the Union's Plan II insurance coverage (as detailed on the SAG website).

By comparison, in the first printing of *The Business of Acting*, in 2002, the minimum figure that needed to be earned was $7,500.

Clearly, this is not becoming a less expensive business to pursue and grow a career in. Aside from the challenges of getting the opportunities, representation and roles you need to build the resume you must have, you are also burdened with how to manage the costs of being and staying a healthy actor—and your union can help you do that, if you are lucky enough to get the opportunities that will bring you to union membership that will also open the doors to the other benefits that come with it.

Now it is time to look at when a new-to-the-business actor should join a union: not right away. Put it off for as long as you can.

If you are a new actor, your goal should be to generate opportunities to build your resume, to make contacts and connections, and to develop your talent and skills. Aside from training and classes, you can only achieve these things by actually working in acting jobs.

There are a lot of opportunities for nonunion actors to work in a myriad of productions all over the country that would not be open to them if they were union members. Yes, the union's stronghold is in the protection of actors' minimums, and yes, nonunion productions rarely pay actors at the same rates that union work does. However, as you build your career, it is the experiences you gain, not how much you get paid (or even *if* you get paid), that are valuable.

As you build your resume, you will never put next to the acting credit whether the role was a union or nonunion job, and you will never list how much (if anything) you were paid for it. So, if it is experience and opportunity that count (and I believe that they *do* count a lot), then the rest of it does not matter—both in the beginning and in the long run.

The level of competition for roles can be quite different in the nonunion arena, as well. Since every actor wants to be in the union, and since once you are in the union you are prohibited from working on and in nonunion projects, there will be many actors who are unable to audition for these parts that you might be very right for.

As you build your resume, you will grow both your ability and your potential. You will nurture your talent and you will build your confidence from your opportunities to work.

You will know when and if it is the right time to become union-affiliated. But remember, no union will serve you better than you will or should serve yourself.

Prestige by association? Hardly.

Just because an actor is a member of a union, it does not mean that he or she is any more talented, experienced or qualified to work than any nonunion actor—and just because you have gained union status does not mean that great things will happen right away (if ever) for your career either, just because you carry a union card. There is a significant managing of expectations that also comes with union membership. Yes, your union card can gain you entry, but it alone will not get you a job.

Your career goals and desires have nothing to do with union membership—and that is important to remember. Achieving your goals requires that you understand your role in the bigger picture of your career and that you develop and utilize the tools and skills that will help you on your journey of achievement. You can do it— and the unions will be there when you are ready for them.

How will you know exactly when? Circumstance and opportunity will guide you. Don't rush it.

With our focus primarily on SAG and AFTRA, it is important to end this part of the discussion with what could happen with both entities moving forward.

The unions will always be significant players in the business of acting. While the landscape in which they all operate has changed, their survival will be rooted in their ability to adapt to the needs of their members in both the new and future environments.

When my first book was published, there were talks about merging SAG and AFTRA into one mega-union that could better serve the membership of both organizations. Of course it never happened.

The recurring outcry over the years from activist SAG leaders (and actors) was, in general, that they did not want a union (AFTRA) whose primary jurisdiction and concerns included soap operas, local newscasters and radio broadcasters having a hand (or a say) in contracts for network television and feature film work by actors. With SAG being the larger of the two unions in membership numbers (SAG has approximately 120,000 members, AFTRA approximately 70,000), passage of a move to merge was defeated.

That was then.

The landscape has since changed. Projects that were once considered to be the domain of SAG have now become AFTRA-ruled; the proliferation of new media production has seen projects and producers divided over which union ends up sanctioning them. As those waters become murkier and as the competition for grabbing projects to one side or the other becomes greater, my prediction is that, in time, the leadership and the members of both unions will come to realize that in the new business of acting, much more can be achieved that benefits all members by working together than can ever be achieved by continuing to work against each other.

That has already begun to happen. While both unions split on the theatrical contract negotiations that fractured the industry in the last go-around, they have since come together to negotiate and pass a new commercial contract that serves all members and both unions well.

Moving into the future, it does not have to be newscaster vs. actor. An AFTRA-SAG merger can, in the process, create appropriate divisions that specialize in the needs that are specific to a class, designation or category that a member falls into. Often times, professional artists (be they actor or broadcaster) fall into more than one classification. The actor as talk show host? I'm sure that Ellen DeGeneres is happy to claim membership in both unions, as are approximately 50,000 other industry professionals.

Another piece of the future union puzzle remains unclear. The official relationship between the Association of Talent Agents (the organization that represents more than 100 talent agencies in Los Angeles and New York) and SAG is currently nonexistent. Franchise agreements between SAG and ATA members, which sanctioned these agencies as approved and worthy of representing SAG actors, expired nearly a decade ago. This agreement sought to standardize and limit, at its core, the commission rate a SAG actor would pay to his or her agent at ten percent. It also put limits on franchised agencies with regard to how and under what certain conditions these agencies needed to operate.

As the business landscape began to shift in 2002, ATA member agencies were interested in growing their own business interests, as well as their clients'—and sought changes to the soon-toexpire franchise agreement with SAG that would allow them this flexibility.

SAG's position was that the changes ATA member agencies sought would or could create a conflict of interest or otherwise affect an agency's allegiance and/or its ability to fully represent actor clients. The process to negotiate a new franchise agreement fell apart and, as of this writing, one is still not in place.

While SAG offers up a list of franchised agents on their website, this list represents individual talent agencies, not the ATA itself, that have made individual agreements with the union.

In the day-to-day business of acting, this amounts to very little for a union (or nonunion) actor to be concerned with. For a time, some talent agencies were, in place of a SAG-franchised contract with their clients, asking clients, instead, to sign a General Services Agreement for representation, which would allow the agency to collect a greater rate of commission, up to 20 percent in California (the limit was held at ten percent in New York). Some actors signed these GSAs as asked; others were smart enough to negotiate those terms. Most agencies held to a ten percent cap.

Since then, the ATA has a franchise agreement in place with AFTRA.

Interestingly enough, even as the new business of acting has seen a tremendous growth in the business of talent management, neither union has sought to create or even discuss a franchise agreement between talent managers and any of these organizations.

If a talent union seeks to protect and advocate for the best interests of their members, adapting to the needs of the new and future landscape must include the acknowledgement, the recognition, the embracing and the encouragement of the work done by legitimate talent managers that growing numbers of their members benefit from. At the end of each union member's dues calculating period, the union should not care how a member got a job, but instead, that the member was able to secure work, build their resume, add to their bank account and, where the bottom line is always the bottom line, increase the revenue the union sees when their members get hired and paid to work.

At the very least, it is an exploratory committee that both AFTRA and SAG leadership should create. I am more than willing to serve on it and would eagerly be involved in any way I can, if asked.

We all need to move the future of this business smartly and strategically ahead to serve the best interests of all parties involved.

CHAPTER 8

AN ACTOR'S RESUME & BIO:

Creating Critical Work-In-Progress Tools That Define Your Unique Brand and Your Potential

THERE IS NOTHING that makes more of a statement about what kind of actor you are now and what kind of actor you have the potential to become than a smartly crafted, well-worded, truthful resume.

I know of at least two talent agents who not only ask, but encourage, their new-to-the-business actor clients to pad their resumes to make them look better and the clients appear more experienced than they really are. I could not disagree with this practice more.

No actor is born with a SAG card (yet) or a resume (yet). Everyone starts at where you are supposed to, which is at the beginning. Whereas a SAG card is a privilege you earn, so, too, is your education, your training and your work credits.

I hate liars. Lying on a resume is rooted in lack of self-confidence and incredible, entitled nerve. Rather than be seen for exactly who and what they are (young actors with great potential), many young people think it is better to pad the early evidence of a career in their favor. They could not be doing themselves a greater disservice.

In the managing expectations department alone, the truths of your resume inform a prospective agent and manager (or casting director) the information needed to manage their expectations of what you already know and what you still need to learn.

If you cannot yet walk a tightrope, we would never submit you for an acting job that would have you doing that unless and until we knew that you could do it safely and were professionally trained to do so. We would never submit you for a Shakespeare festival play unless you really were trained and prepared to play a Shakespearean role. We would not set you up to audition for a musical unless you really can sing and dance (and sing and dance not just well, but sing and dance brilliantly). So do not pretend that you can, unless you *really* can.

Worse than submitting a photo that does not look like you, then getting called in for an audition or a meeting because of that photo (a meeting that will generally not go well for anyone involved), putting credits on your resume that you have not (yet) earned just to make yourself look more experienced than you presently are will also get you in trouble.

I once had an actor who had contacted me about seeking management come in for a meeting for possible representation. I was not as much interested in signing him as I was eager to teach him an important lesson before he lied himself out a career.

When his photo and resume arrived in the mail a few weeks earlier, in reviewing it, I could not help but notice a credit he had listed on his resume for a theatrical production that, unbeknownst to him, I had been a producer of. This young man claimed to have appeared in that production. I, of course, knew better. He was not in it.

During our meeting, when I gingerly pressed him on it, he finally admitted that his cousin had worked in the box office at the theatre where the production took place. Enough said. I don't even think he saw the show, which was an out-of-town production. He probably figured, "Who would ever know?" You never know. I did.

Is it a lie to call yourself a co-star of a project that you were really just an extra in? Is it really a lie to list that you have had training in Elizabethan improv when you have not even taken a standard improv class? Is it a lie to proclaim on your resume that you are fluent in Spanish when all you can do is say "Hola" and order tacos in a Mexican restaurant? Yes, yes and yes.

Many young and/or new actors worry that the acting resume they come out of college and/or enter the business with is not enough to attract the attention of anyone in the industry who might represent or cast them—and they would be right.

It is your job coming into this business to ensure that your action plan is rooted in preparing you for the journey ahead—and that includes professional training, professional classes and professional coaching to balance what you have learned academically in school with the real-life requirements of being a professional actor.

Your resume should always paint an accurate picture of the work you have already done and the training you have already had on the road to your becoming a complete, ready-to-be-working actor.

Where your acting credits are light or nonexistent, balance them or infuse your clean slate with a detailed list of the acting-related classes you have taken in school and the professional training you have begun to receive. For a wanting-to-be-working actor, there is no excuse not to be in a professional class on a regular basis. In fact, I insist that you do so.

Currently taking or having recently taken an ongoing class or workshop with a respected industry teacher will score you a lot of points from those of us whose attention you seek to gain. You may not have had the opportunity to work professionally yet, but that is not your fault. However, there is no excuse not to train, not to study, not to stretch, not to learn, not to explore.

Many well-respected casting directors offer excellent workshops that provide one-time or short-term opportunities for actors of all ages and at all stages of their careers to learn important skills that can propel their careers forward. What better way to learn audition technique than from a person who auditions actors for a living?

It is also a great opportunity to take the fear out of the process by watching and experiencing first-hand how a casting director works. Seeing that process deconstructed before your eyes can be very empowering.

At the same time, watch out for so-called casting directors who work very little or who have very little experience in the business who are trying to supplement their incomes by participating in so-called "pay-to-audition" workshops. They are now illegal in California, but that does not mean they are not still offered. Packaged the right way, you can be offered up almost any service that might otherwise be unlawful.

The pay-to-audition controversy stemmed from a trend whereby certain so-called acting schools would offer up sessions with casting directors that were nothing more than the actor paying an exorbitant fee for the opportunity to be auditioned by a casting director who was under no obligation to teach the actor anything in the process nor hire him for an acting job.

Many an actor who was frustrated by their inability to get auditions (whether they were represented or not) did not give a second thought about paying for a chance to get some face time with a casting director they could not get in to see through the normal route.

At the same time, some casting directors who were eager to earn some extra money started ending the industry practice of having generals (short meetings with actors they did not yet know without having a specific role for them in mind or without their necessarily even casting a project at the time) in their offices in favor of showing up for a one-night session where they could accomplish the same thing and come away with a pocket full of undeclared cash.

Some actors and industry professionals, including some casting directors, began to take issue with this trend.

The State of California stepped in in 2002 and made these types of pay-to-audition workshops illegal and, in the process, established rules, regulations and guidelines for the legitimate schools to adhere to that would ensure the paying participants a valid, valuable and worthy educational experience, not just the opportunity to meet with and audition for a casting director.

These classes and workshops can add up to some great training, if taken at the right schools and with the right teachers. The best way to sort through the large numbers of offerings is to ask your fellow actor friends about workshops and classes they have attended. Postings on public message boards can also serve up some helpful information.

As of this writing, there were lots of opinions offered up on this topic (and others) on the *Back Stage* website message board. The Better Business Bureau is also a good place to check out a school or a class for past complaints filed against the provider. Also, a Google search with the name of the school or business followed by the word "complaint" might also turn up some interesting and helpful information. Do the same for an individual teacher, trainer or coach.

It is important, if you are going to spend your hard-earned (or hard-gifted) dollars on any independent, professional class, coach, seminar or workshop, that you are investing in yourself and not helping to line the pockets of providers who are more interested in their bottom lines than they are in your career, your action plan or helping you develop your career potential.

Many coaches who offer ongoing classes are eager to offer potential new students the opportunity to sit in and audit a class before you make both the financial and time commitment. Some will, some will not. Either way, it is always a smart request to make before signing up and paying out.

Classes taken with respected teachers or at respected post-college professional facilities can greatly enhance a resume that is rather light on or entirely lacking in professional credits. It is important to prove to a potential agent or manager that you are not just an actor waiting for an opportunity that the agent or manager might deliver, but that, instead, even though you are new, or young or reinventing yourself, you are being proactive about being trained, prepared and ready for the opportunities that you will together generate through your business partnership.

Creating Your Resume

You can review some resume samples at TheBusinessOfActing.com that can serve as templates for the creation of your own resume. I am not as concerned about format, per se, as I am about content.

The basics include:

+ Keep your resume to one page, no matter how many credits or how much information you have to list. As recent credits get pushed down the list in favor of current credits, when the time comes that they do not fit on a single page, edit them out, unless, of course, one of these credits is for a role, a project or work with a prominent director that makes it noteworthy and of value. Then, keep it as a part of your visible resume for a long as it makes sense to do so.

+ Font size should never be less than 12 point on your hard copy resume; font sizes on the professional self-submission services is pre-selected for you.

+ Depending on your age, it is perfectly okay, on your first professional resume, to include high school and college productions that you have performed in; just label them as such. However, if you are over 25, I would leave the high school stuff out and, once you pass 30, it is a good time to dump the college stuff, too. Besides, you will need the space for all of the additional professional credits you will have accumulated.

+ Call your role what it was. If it was an under five (five lines or less), do not inflate it to co-star status. If it was a supporting role, do not promote yourself to a lead. If it was an extra role, it does not belong on your resume at all, unless your acting career goal is to be a professional career extra, which many union (and nonunion) actors alike are, making better-than-entry-level job pay in the process of having this specific career.

+ In the Personal category (and there should always be a Personal category), list your height and weight—and your *real* height and weight. No one reviewing your resume is making any personal judgments about you. If a casting director is looking for a particular (body) type, this information can get you in. Particularly in a landscape where the submitted image of you that they are looking at is a thumbnail head shot and not a body shot, these accurate statistics are very important to include.

+ The biggest stretches in provided information on an actor's resume (even outright lies) can almost always be found in the Special Skills section. If you are not fluent in French, but, instead, only know a few words or phrases, do not list that you can speak the language. If you cannot do anything more than play "Chopsticks" on the piano, do not list that you can play that instrument. On the other hand, if you are good at card tricks, magic, trampoline jumping or speed texting, include it.

While special skills may not always or necessarily be significant in your being called in for a film, television or stage role, it is almost always an essential part of the commercial casting process.

When creating your resume profile on sites such as ActorsAccess .com or CastingNetworks.com, there is significant time required to complete the Special Skills section. In greater detail than you might imagine possible (or necessary), providing this information honestly, accurately and completely can open the doors to audition opportunities simply because you possess specific skills.

You will not being judged on how much you can do, in general, just on whether you can deliver when asked to do something specific that sets you apart from the bigger pool of actors in your category or of your type.

Let's spend a moment on extra work. It is a large part of the business of acting, and while computer-generated extras can take up a lot of space in some films, like *Avatar*, for example, real people (read: real actors), thankfully, are still widely used to create the atmosphere and background of television episodes and feature films.

If you are not going after a career as a professional extra, doing extra work in the beginning of your career, or even from time to time for a while thereafter, can be a good experience, if your ego is comfortable with it and if you are doing it for the right reasons.

You will *not* get discovered by the director while working as an extra and be bumped up to a lead role. But if your exposure to a production set has been limited or nonexistent, doing extra work will provide you with an opportunity to see how the process works from as close a vantage point as you can get—and get paid for it.

It is also a great way to meet other actors and people in some production-related jobs. But if you seek work as an extra, you should not work those jobs for social interaction and/or contacts alone. Rather, you should see extra work as a part of your continuing education in your early career journey.

There are casting directors and casting agencies who only work in the business of securing extras for film and television productions. The names of reputable, legitimate companies that do this specific work are available from SAG and AFTRA (and elsewhere).

Casting directors who are hired to cast the speaking roles in a production usually do not hire the extras. An agency that specializes in extra casting generally gets those assignments.

In order to be a successful extra (again, unless your goal is to be a career extra), you have to know when to stop doing extra work. Indeed, many actors make good livings as professional extras, sometimes even as regular extras on a television series, but making this choice requires a commitment that can make the pursuit of other acting opportunities difficult, if not impossible.

I do not believe that extra work should be listed on your resume, unless you are or want to be a professional extra. Likewise, I have never met a casting director who thinks extra work counts in the building of a long-term acting career. But I do not think anyone would argue the value that the opportunity for exposure to the process can give a smart actor, even if only temporarily.

Whether it is a union or nonunion job, the exposure is all the same. It is just how much you get paid for your time that varies (and there can be a huge difference between a union and nonunion extra job).

An acting job should never be about the money it generates, only the opportunity it affords you, which numerous times in the early stages of a career can frequently mean great opportunity, but no pay.

The focus needs to be on building your professional resume, not on passing up the opportunity for an acting job simply because of the lack of a paycheck, which is why a "survival" job is such a necessity.

Student films, 99-seat theatre, independent films, classes, workshops, seminars, coaching and fully embracing any and every opportunity to hone your skills and become better at your craft—and smarter at running your business—will keep both your action plan and your career journey moving in the right direction.

Your honest, work-in-progress resume, more than anything else in the early stages of your career, will define to a potential agent, manager or casting director how serious you are about achieving success in the business of acting.

CREATING YOUR ACTING BIO

A bio is a handy tool for every actor to have. Knowing how to write one is also an important skill to master. At the very least, each time you appear in a theatrical production, you will be asked to supply one for the production's program. Sometimes casting directors and prospective representatives will request a brief bio, too, along with your photo and resume materials. Having this material available on your website is also a great way to market yourself and your brand.

To create a full-fledged biography, you could easily end up with a multi-page, hard-copy document. That is not what this assignment is about. This assignment instead, is about creating a brief story, a profile of you, highlighting your acting career achievements so far. It is about painting a picture of who you are as an actor that is presented interestingly enough to make someone want to know more about you—or to pay attention to your work.

The longer your career, the more you will have worked; the older you become, the more experience you will get. As you grow professionally, so will your bio. Keep it current. As with your resume, add new credits as you earn them; take out older credits as they become less important as your career develops.

The assignment I am giving you is to create your own bio, to complement your newly created, work-in-progress, professional resume. You will find some format suggestions below. You will also find some sample bios to reference as templates on our website, at TheBusinessOfActing.com.

Your hard copy bio should not run more than one page, double-spaced, and ideally, it will only be a few paragraphs.

The bios that I write for my clients that are hard-copy printed (or pdf file-ready for e-mailing or uploading) are always headlined with the name of the person, in all caps, centered, in bold and in

16-point font. Centered directly under the person's name, in bold, 14-point, upper and lowercase, I simply type the word "Biography" (without the quotes). The rest of the document is double-spaced, left and right margins justified, paragraphs indented and in 12-point font.

I use several bio versions for my clients, depending on the need for the bio and my intention for giving it to the person requesting it or the person to whom I am proactively sending it.

If it is for a *Playbill*-type publication for a cast member profile in a play's program, I submit the shorter version, one that highlights only the most important and interesting aspects of the actor and his career. On the other hand, if the bio is to be used to prepare a reporter, talk show host or researcher for a publicity interview, I send the most detailed bio I have available to provide the most useful, current, accurate and interesting information as possible.

For a bio that is to be used on a website (yours or someone else's), use your best judgment in uploading a document that is easy to read on a computer screen or other device and that says just enough, but not too much.

Check out the sample bios on our website to help get you started.

There is a fine art to creating effective, professional resumes and bios—and an important part of that process is to always keep in mind that each of these documents is a key business tool that is intended to help you create an awareness of yourself, your brand, your experience, your training and your potential.

CHAPTER 9

EMOTIONAL, PHYSICAL AND FISCAL
FITNESS IN THE NEW LANDSCAPE

A HAPPY, HEALTHY ACTOR is a much better person to work with. Just ask any happy, healthy actor. Too often actors bury the angst they feel from stuff in their lives that they have no control over and project it places where it does not belong. Money also matters in the business of acting. Not the mega-millions you will one day earn, but the dollars you need for your survival now.

Before you can take care of business, it is essential that you take care of yourself at every level. Your action plan must cover three key areas that are often neglected by new and experienced actors alike. They are emotional, physical and fiscal fitness.

Let's look at each category separately and see why they are each vitally important.

EMOTIONAL FITNESS

How you feel about yourself has a direct connection with how you relate to the world and how the world relates back to you. Self-confidence matters, self-esteem matters and the belief that you are worthy of the success you seek matters.

The state of your emotional fitness can impact how you audition, if you even get the opportunity to audition, how you perform when given the opportunity and how you interact with others. This includes your friends, your family, your colleagues, your representatives, casting directors and, of course, other actors. In short, everyone.

Actors are likely people to take most things that happen to them and around them personally. Because so much of the work you do (or will do) requires you to create an emotional life for a character you play, it is practically a requirement to be able to locate and access all kinds of emotions, some deep within you, others closer to the surface, in your goal to truly create and inhabit a role.

When not needing to utilize this library of stored emotions, it is important to learn how not to let situations and circumstances you will find yourself in push the buttons in you that trigger an emotional, often negative, response as you implement and grow your action plan.

The three biggest emotions you will need to work hard to avoid, to tame and to conquer, are states of desperation, disappointment and a sense of entitlement, all of which can easily slip you into a depressive, frustrated, angry and/or cynical state of mind. It is not healthy and it is a counterproductive place from which to operate your business, build your career and steer your journey. It also does not make you a very pleasant person to be around under any circumstance.

Decisions that are made about you in, from, during or after an audition are not about you at all. Decisions on who gets cast are based on factors that are, usually, completely out of your control. So why then should you pay an emotional price for that decision? The answer is, you should not.

Being disappointed about not getting a role you really want or representation by that manager or agent you thought would be a good match for you is a normal reaction. Go ahead and experience it, but then quickly regroup and move on.

Unless your behavior in an audition or in any other business meeting or situation was inappropriate or otherwise off the professional mark, there is no blame to assign, nor is there a result to spin, whether in your own mind or in conversations with others about what you have been through.

You cannot and should not claim responsibility for something you did not do or did not cause. Actors often look to potential opportunities that did not come to them or that were lost along the way as something to beat themselves up about. This is nonsense.

Learn from your experiences, do not burn from them. Work at *not* being too hard on yourself when things you wish would happen have not yet, through no fault of your own, occurred. Work at *not* feeling personally responsible for the opportunities you feel you do not get. Instead, be proud of the small achievements you do accumulate. They really do matter as you build both your career and your self-confidence.

If you become and remain an empowered, proactive actor at every point of your career journey, the opportunities that are meant to be yours will come to you.

In the meantime, it is critical to have the kind of balance in your life that gives both meaning to your life and fulfillment to you personally, without the need to find that joy in getting an audition or in booking a job. Balance is essential. It makes you a well-rounded person. It gives you much-needed time off from the pursuit of your career. It fills your life with the perspective that you come away with after spending quality time with family you love and friends you care about.

In the Business of Acting class, each semester features a series of in-class meetings that students have with a variety of industry professionals, including working actors.

One of these guests on the regular lineup is my long-time client and friend Pamela Roylance. As a 50+ working actor, her story of early success in series television, followed by a career movement stall, followed by career success again, is an empowering one to hear, to absorb and to embrace.

I want my students to understand that most actors are having lives and careers exactly like Pamela's. The expectation or anticipation among most young actors is that the business of acting is just waiting for them to complete their academic educations and then career success will quickly open up to them.

While this may be true for a select few, it is hardly how real life plays itself out for most actors. Even if opportunity finds you early in your journey, there is no guarantee that success will stick around or that a fresh opportunity will come to you right away when the job you have landed, whether series, film, commercial or play, ends—and, sooner or later, they all end.

Actress Isabel Sanford is a great case in point. While television audiences remember her from her Emmy Award-winning role as Louise Jefferson on the long-running hit comedy *The Jeffersons*, most do not know that Isabel's career success (read: fame and fortune) came to her much later in life. While she was, indeed, living the life of a working actor, with a day job to pay the bills and support her family as a single parent and appearing in countless plays at night, it was not until she was in her fifties that the kind of success we think of as having "made it" came to her.

Long after the time that most people would have simply given up, she came to the opportunity that would—and did—change her life for the rest of her life.

Of course, she would have preferred that success and money come to her from her work as an actor earlier in her life, but she was smart enough to hold on to her dream and pursue her passion because she *had* to—and that is my point.

Pursue this career because you *have* to. Pursue this career because this is, at your core, what you have to do. Do not ever, under any circumstances, pursue this career because you seek the fame, notoriety and money that success might deliver to you, but, instead, because your own passion tells you that you are prepared to both make the compromises the commitment will ask of you and to wait for it to be your time.

This falls into the managing expectations category.

A young client of mine called me the other day to report in on an audition he had gone on. He felt that he was beyond perfect for the role and he left the audition confident that a callback and then an offer to work would soon follow. He was emotionally high coming off what he felt was a great experience. I urged him to embrace, to hold on to and to remember how that feels, because that is exactly how he should feel coming out of *every* audition. Then I urged him to let it go, to forget about that specific audition, but, instead, to retain the confidence that such a high delivers.

Two days passed and there was no contact from the casting director to bring the client in for a callback. When the client called to inquire about it, I gave him the news, to which he responded with tremendous disappointment and frustration.

He just could not understand how he could feel so good about an audition for a part he felt so positive that he nailed that he did not even get a callback for. I reiterated what I have said to him, my other clients and my many students before: it is not about you.

Remember, it is not the best actor who gets the job; it is the *right* actor who gets the part. It is also about a litany of other things that have absolutely nothing to do with you.

In the mix-and-match process that occurs in creating a company of actors for a variety of roles, perhaps the producers decided to go in an ethnic direction that is different from yours. Perhaps they went older or younger. Perhaps they changed the gender of the role. It does not matter much, because in the black-and-white world that is the new business of acting, you either get the role or you do not. There is nothing murky about it—and to attempt to seek out the reasons why or why not is not helpful. You just have to move on.

Here is that mantra again: the value of any audition is not in getting the job. Making a positive impression is the goal. If you accomplish that, there will be no emotional damage to suffer or consequences to pay the price for.

And while we are talking about how to ensure an emotionally fit audition when that opportunity does come your way, it is important for you to have something else planned to do immediately after every audition. Meet a friend for coffee. Go to the gym. Take a yoga class. Go for a walk.

Have something to do instead of sitting around thinking about your audition and waiting, hoping, for your cell phone to ring or a text message to arrive with the news you hope for. Having something else to do, something to take your mind off of your audition, will help you put the experience exactly where the experience belongs—within you, not consuming you.

Careers begin to happen when talent, training, preparedness and readiness meet good luck and opportunity—and not until then. That is why you must be prepared for the long haul. That is why it is so important to find and explore a passion in something else that will also feed your creative spirit and honor your ambition.

Survival in the new business of acting requires that you plan, prepare and stick to a system that will keep you fed, housed, trained and ready.

This client I mentioned earlier also raised an interesting question. Being a fairly new-to-the-business actor and now experiencing what it is like to get auditions and callbacks, but no bookings (yet), his frustration generated the question, "Well, I understand that I may not be the right actor, but when will it be my turn to make great art?" My response: The business of acting is not about making great art; it is about making money.

For most producers, studios and production companies, it is usually about spending as little as one can to generate as much as one can. Create high art on your own; produce your own digital film, write your own stage play or one-person show, take a sculpting class.

With the exception of a handful of projects each year, Hollywood is about box office figures and ratings.

It is not my intention to be unsupportive of this client or his ambition to make both a statement and a difference through the acting work he wants to do. Rather, it is my intent to paint a realistic picture of the new business of acting, which, like the old business of acting, is almost always about the bottom line.

It is very early in his career journey. My client will undoubtedly find the balance he is seeking to become a working actor, to feel fulfilled from and by his art, and be inspired by the opportunities he can create to both make money and feel emotionally fit.

It is easy to fall into the trap of comparing the opportunities that do not come your way to that friend of yours, who happens to be your same type, who seems to get out on a lot more roles than you do. This behavior will get you nowhere fast.

There will be plenty of times during the journey of your career that you get opportunities that others will find easy to envy. Keep focused on your job at hand, which is to grow and nurture both your brand and your business. While it is perhaps somewhat important for McDonald's to have an awareness of what Burger King is up to, McDonald's needs to follow its own strategic plan without regard to what it deems to be the competition.

For our Web TV series *Inside the Business of Acting* (InsideThe BusinessOfActing.com), I interviewed many successful, working actors and other industry professionals about their careers, their turning points and the lessons they learned along the way. The goal of this series is to enlighten, to educate and to empower a global audience of young, new-to-the-business actors in the journeys of their own careers.

Emotional fitness has played—and continues to play—a vital role in the careers of the many people featured in this series. There are many words of caution and advice to the novice actor in these interviews that are clear, concise and very worthy of underscoring.

Hal Linden, the Tony- and Emmy Award-winning actor who starred in the long-running ABC-TV series *Barney Miller* (1975—1982) was emphatic in his warning to young actors. He said, "This business is too difficult. It should only be entered into by people who can't do anything else. Not (for the person) who *wants* to be in show business, but (for the person) who *must* be in show business."

His point is, as he emphatically stated, "You have to be prepared never to succeed—and it was only the journey that was worth it."

I couldn't agree more.

Tony-nominated Broadway and television star Bonnie Franklin whose series *One Day at a Time* ran on CBS-TV for nine years (1975–1984) also talked about how to prepare for the emotional roller coaster that comes with a career as an actor. She was heartfelt in offering up her perspective and echoed a lot of what Hal Linden said.

"If there is something else you want to do or something else you enjoy doing, then do it," Bonnie said. She cautioned, "You have to be able to take rejection because you are rejected most of the time and then you have to keep picking yourself up and going back to it. You better have a passion for what it is you do—and a *real* passion, that there isn't anything you can do or want to do or can live without because…it's murder. It's murder, very often on family, it's murder on your soul…and the benefits are there, if you're lucky enough to reap those benefits—and when you have one of those moments on stage or on television when it all works, it's like magic. But, most of the time, it's just work."

So much for seeking high art.

Even when you are lucky enough to work, you may often find that the quality of work you are asked to do is not fulfilling, it is not stimulating, it is, as Bonnie Franklin put it," just work."

But, looking at it another way, so what? It is an acting job that you landed because you were the right actor for the role.

Your action plan must be built around a strategy of always looking and always moving forward, to borrow the title of Bonnie's hit series, one day at a time.

Not every day will feel as though great progress has been made—and that is okay. The goal is to do at least one positive, proactive thing every day in support of your career. While you cannot control what results from your efforts, you can feel the satisfaction that comes from knowing that you are doing everything you know how to do to be a business person of action (not just talk), as well as being actor with a forward-moving (not focused on the past) outlook.

By not relying on anyone else (even when you have representation) and by taking full responsibility for the actions you decide to take or choose not to take, you will ensure that self-doubt, disappointment and what feels like no or little progress at all will be feelings that visit you less and less frequently, and then soon not at all, on your journey to a happy and emotionally fit career.

PHYSICAL FITNESS

An actor has to be fit. Notice I said "fit" and not "in shape." There is a big difference.

What is important is that you recognize the need to take care of yourself. While Hollywood continues to push the "you can't be too thin" message (even in the new business of acting) to vulnerable young teens and others, I hope that you will be smart and ignore that message. Recognize that size, ultimately, does not matter.

Actors are real people. Real people are all sizes and shapes. Real people are portrayed on television, in film and onstage every day. Recognize that you have your own unique look. I do not at all advocate that you change your physical appearance to fit into a Hollywood stereotype. There have always been and there will always be roles for all kinds and sizes and shapes of actors.

I have seen a number of breakdowns lately seeking women aged 50+ with the specific request from the casting directors not to submit anyone who has had Botox. The tide has begun to shift—and that is a very good thing.

Some kind of physical activity (other than jumping to conclusions) should be a part of your life. Your physical fitness, regardless of your body type or size, is important because it can impact your endurance level when you are on a job.

It makes sense to have some kind of regular regimen of cardiovascular exercise. Ride a bike, climb the stairs, go for a walk. An expensive gym membership is not necessary for any of these activities. It is just important that you do something and that you do it regularly.

If you have not exercised since high school gym class (don't laugh—there are tons of people in this category, even thin ones!) or if it has been a while since your last workout, it is always a good idea to get checked out with your doctor before beginning any exercise program at any age. Find out how your blood pressure is. Find out where your cholesterol level lies. Learn where you are on the health and fitness charts and learn to take good care of the vehicle that will deliver your performances to the masses, your body.

There is no doubt that stress can take its toll on you, too, if you let it. While acting itself may not be a stressful career, the act of being an actor and pursing your career, as you may have already experienced, can be very stressful. Taking care of yourself means working at lowering your stress level, too.

While you may not be able to lessen your exposure to it, you can limit the impact stress can have on you. Walking, yoga, Pilates—there is a wide variety of things you can do to promote relaxation. It does not have to cost you a lot or even anything at all. Many communities have high school-located, after-hours curricula where adult or continuing education programs and classes are offered in all kinds of areas, including relaxation techniques. Once you are able to learn how some of these exercises are done, you can re-create them in your own space.

It is easy for actors to fall into the bad habit of thinking they need to be on the go all the time in order for them to advance their careers and to never miss out on any opportunity. That is a self-destructive way of thinking. It is critical to your personal and professional development to recognize the need we all have for some downtime, some quiet time, on a regular basis. The pursuit of your career should not take a toll on you or on the body you need to achieve and maintain goals of success.

That is my definition of physical fitness.

Fiscal Fitness

Part 1: Financial Survival

There has been a growing, unfortunate trend for a while now, fueled by a shifting economy, that has impacted the landscape, whereby the middle class, working actor as a group classification now faces extinction. It was not so long ago that it was very possible to support oneself as a working actor. That is becoming harder and harder for all actors to achieve in the new business of acting.

This shift in the business has resulted in less work for star-level actors who were easily commanding, demanding and getting astronomical salaries for the work they were hired to do. Particularly in television, actors who not so long ago considered themselves "film" actors who would never do television roles are now accepting them.

The domino effect of this change is making it tougher for established, working actors to get the guest star roles that had easily come to them previously.

The "name" actors who take these roles away from the lesser known, working actors who used to get them put many of these other actors in the position of having to take the smaller roles they thought they left behind years ago. The result of this shift is that this level of actor, if he wants to continue to work is, in many cases, forced to go up for the roles that were once the territory of the young and new-to-the-business actor, roles on which young and new careers were built.

This struggle has also had an enormous fiscal impact on a talent agency or management company whose working clients had long delivered the level of commissions any agency needs to survive. When actors are paid less, everyone on their team pays the price.

You must recognize that make a living in the new business of acting is a tough objective. Of course it can be done and many do it. But the financial struggles many of these actors have endured before this happens (and that many endure again after the projects they are in are finished and when no other acting job immediately follows) is a constant reminder that you must be fiscally strategic and financially smart if you intend to stick around.

The very mention of "fiscal responsibility" is enough to bring on a panic attack in many people, particularly if you are recently out of school. Recent graduates usually find themselves facing pressure from their parents to get a job and earn money. Added to that is the pressure they put on themselves to get started with their chosen careers. It is also common to begin to feel overwhelmed, having just been dumped out into the real world by the school, college or university you graduated from. I hear this a lot.

Whether you are just entering the real world or have been surviving in it for years, your fiscal fitness is vital to your health and to your career.

The three rules of fiscal fitness are:
1) You have to live somewhere and be able to pay for it.
2) You have to eat regularly and be able to pay for it.
3) There is a minimum amount of money that you must earn first to survive and then to thrive.

Our discussion of finances falls into two categories: living expenses and career expenses. But, first, let me offer up what I hope you will think is a creative fiscal approach, particularly for students soon to (or who will eventually) graduate from college. I call it The Business of Acting Gift Registry®.

Here is how it works:

Lots of graduates get gifted by (mostly) relatives who want to acknowledge in some way the achievement of earning a degree. I like the intent from where this gifting comes, but I would like to suggest that you be proactive and strategic about not just planting seeds or giving hints, but by coming right out and asking for gifts of support that can (and usually will) be enormously helpful to you as you embark out into the real world on your own, ready to establish your post-college life and launch the action plan for your career.

Instead of coming away from graduation with gifts that will not really serve you, why not come away from this accomplishment with both your degree *and* some "seed" money to get you started?

Almost immediately, you will need to have a head shot session with a professional photographer. You will also need the funds to create accounts and build your self-submission casting profiles on the various industry services. You will need to start taking professional-level classes to bridge your academic training from college with the training necessary to get you ready to compete in the professional marketplace (and then keep your acting skills sharp and improving).

Of course, all of this costs money—and here is where The Business of Acting Gift Registry® comes in.

Instead of taking away gifts, take away cash. Ask for cash contributions instead of other gifts that you can use to fund these real-need items. Those who gift you will feel a deeper sense of being supportive of you at every level if they know that they have helped you invest in your future.

Make a list of the first-step items you will need to fund and then circulate it to family, friends, anyone appropriate who would not feel put on the spot or uncomfortable being in your gift registry loop. While one person alone may not write you a check to fully cover that first professional photo session, it can be a contribution toward reaching your fundraising goals.

Whatever cash or checks you receive, deposit them into a new bank account you create just for this purpose. Then, as you are personally able, add to this fund yourself, even a little at a time.

As you begin to incur the expenses of your action plan and career launch, pay them from this account. This will help you keep your personal expenses separate from your business expenses, as well as give you a dedicated account to build on as you begin to earn income from either your acting work, your career support job or both.

By the way, The Business of Acting Gift Registry® is not exclusively for people graduating from school. Designate financial gifts received for other occasions, like birthdays, to a designated account and reap the rewards of planning for (and then being able to cover) your career financial needs.

I was particularly impressed when two of my former students announced their intent to marry and then instead of registering at some random department store or home furnishing chain, created a Business of Acting Wedding Gift Registry® to suggest to their family and friends ways to gift them for their wedding that would both celebrate their union and support their newly launched mutual careers in the business of acting. I thought this was a great, creative idea. They sent thank you notes of the backs of their new head shots. That has to be a first!

It is not the norm, nor is it reasonable, to think that you will complete school and then land a series or a big movie deal within the first month after graduation. As much as we would all like for that to be the case, don't count on it. So what do you do? How do you live? How can you get by financially without compromising the start of your career and the pursuit of those opportunities?

Depending on your age, you have more or less financial responsibility on your plate. If you are in your thirties, forties, fifties or beyond, it is a different picture than if you are in your twenties and just starting out. These rules, however, still apply regardless of your age or stage of life. It is not easy. But if you remain focused on your long-term goals and stick to your personal action plan, you can do it.

You have probably heard about or know actors who live in Los Angeles or New York who take jobs as waiters or waitresses or in some other kind of minimum-wage work in order to support themselves between auditions and acting jobs. Maybe you have already done exactly this yourself. You probably are also aware that many actors take on temp jobs through an employment agency while pursuing their professional careers. You may have already had experience with this process, as well.

If you have to have a job while your career comes together (and often even thereafter), then securing a work assignment in an environment that is conducive to what you want to do with your life can be extremely beneficial to you in logging personal achievements and a lot of exposure.

If you are in Los Angeles or New York (and many cities in between), temp jobs at entertainment companies, studios, ad agencies, or publicity or casting offices can provide you with both dollars and valuable experience. These jobs can also open doors for you to connections and opportunity.

But, many times, this is not enough. In the early stages of your career (and even later on), you will find yourself doing a lot of acting without compensation. Sometimes it is a role you really want to play and have not had the opportunity to do so before. Sometimes it is a favor for a friend. Often, it is simply an opportunity to continue to build on your resume, keep your credits current, keep your acting skills honed and keep moving forward on your journey.

At the end of the day, at the end of the week, at the end of each month, there are and will be bills to pay and those responsibilities must be tended to first. Rent, food, transportation, classes, head shots, career resources, personal entertainment and pure fun times with friends all need to be funded. Some are critical necessities; others, of course, are not.

The truth is that no one likes a hungry actor, both literally and figuratively speaking. A casting director can spot a hungry actor in any audition room because "hungry," often, also means desperate, as in the line from *A Chorus Line,* "I really need this job."

Agents and managers can also spot a hungry actor. It is the actor who is trying too hard be what he or she thinks the agent or manager (or casting director) wants them to be. They have allowed their mismanaged financial situation and the pursuit of the career they dream of having to get in the way of taking care of themselves in ways that can deliver the career they seek, not derail them off their action plan.

An actor acts, yes. An actor also studies and trains when she is not working. And before any actor can do any of this, she must have the funds in place to support herself and the costs of launching, maintaining and building her career.

Finding non-acting work that does not turn you bitter is crucial. Too often I meet angry actors who have gotten themselves stuck in non-acting jobs that drain their energy and deplete their spirit for the work in developing the career they want.

Work at not allowing yourself to get to that place. Instead, prevent anger from setting in by first being smart.

Temporary jobs are plentiful in major cities such as New York and Los Angeles. Even in a bruised economy where layoffs are more the norm than permanent hires, temps are routinely getting called in to fill the jobs that need to be done at rates and under circumstances that are better for many businesses to tolerate and fund than the cost of a full-time hire.

I encourage actors to seek temp jobs through agencies who do not charge a fee for their services to the applicant. There are many temporary staffing agencies in both New York and Los Angeles that cater specifically to the entertainment industry. If the paying acting job you are aching for has not arrived yet, what better place to put in your non-acting work hours than in another part of the industry in which you intend to build your career?

I also meet plenty of actors who have turned their entrepreneurial skills into great outside business opportunities for themselves. Many of my own clients have launched successful ventures ranging from computer and tech services to website design and home interior decorating. Others teach in drama programs for kids. Still others cannot resist the low stress impact (and the joy, for many, of health insurance) available by working at a nearby Starbucks.

A young client of mine called me recently to share the good news that he had just landed a job at his neighborhood Starbucks. I took that as a good move for this particular client whose shortage of funds was preventing him from being able to take the professional classes he needed to be in.

If you have a passion for creative work of another kind, pursue it. If you do not, go out and find what else it is that interests you and do that work.

I have met actors who are quick to offer up an argument against taking jobs in any area other than acting. They will ask, "What happens when I get an audition?" "What if taking the time off to go on an audition would be a problem where I work?"

I respond by asking them how they plan to survive financially if they do not work. I also offer up a solution.

The answer is simple, if you just consider the hard facts. This is not meant to be discouraging, only realistic. The odds that you will be called for an audition more than once every week or two are rare for most actors. I am not saying that it cannot or does not happen. What I am saying is that it is not the rule for most actors.

Even for more experienced actors, auditions (or offers to work) do not come as often as you might think they do (commercial auditions are a different story; more about that shortly).

When an opportunity does present itself for an audition, it is all in how you manage your time.

Do the best you can to schedule that appointment during your lunch break. Take an earlier or later lunch, if you have to or if you can. If you will need a little extra time, ask if you can stay late to make it up.

It is important to tell any employer right from the start that you are an actor and that, from time to time, an audition will come up that may take you away from the office, the restaurant, the store, etc. Tell them, too, that you intend to have those appointments scheduled so as not to interfere with your responsibilities or your schedule at work whenever possible.

I have never known an employer to tell actors/employees who were upfront and honest about their situation that they could not work it out. Besides, if one of these auditions turns into a job that turns out to be that golden opportunity you have been working toward, then you won't need the job you took time off from to make that audition anyway.

See how it all works out?

Commercial auditions can be a little trickier if you do not plan ahead.

Commercial agents are generally given blocks of time ("windows") by commercial casting directors during which time frame the actors who are selected by that agent to audition can come in. When your commercial agent contacts you with an audition appointment for a specific time, if you have a true conflict, ask what the "window" is. Usually it is broad enough so that you can go within a range of hours that should not interfere with your work schedule or that you can work around.

Do not be afraid to speak up and ask (or e-mail) your agent that question. Actors can tend to become so intimidated by their agents, or so afraid of annoying them, that when they do get a call for an audition, the last thing they want to do is risk what they think would be ticking off the agent and appearing ungrateful by asking questions.

You have a responsibility to yourself and to the career you are building to ask any and all questions you need to or want to ask about any audition, including the time it takes place, so do it.

By the way, it is a good idea to keep a small collection of clothing items in your car. What if you are in jeans and your last-minute audition later today is for a character in a business suit? I have never heard of an actor who lost out on a job because of wardrobe. But, nonetheless, to appear dressed in something appropriate for the role you are auditioning for does not hurt. I think it helps.

You should also make it a habit to write down or somewhere enter in exactly what it is that you wear to every audition. When you get a callback, you are usually expected to return looking exactly as you did when you were first seen. Writing down what you wore will save your available brain space for line memorization, not wardrobe reflection, particularly if the callback is many days or weeks after your first audition, which can happen.

You will avoid ever feeling stuck or in a rut if you continue to follow your commitment to your plan and your responsibility to do at least one thing that is both positive and proactive in the interest of your career every day.

There have been plenty of stories in the media about once megarich stars who claim to be broke, having spent and spent and spent, either stupidly or foolishly, or who never sought the advice of (or listened to) more fiscally responsible people.

Just because you are making money in the business of acting is no reason to start spending it. Plan for the future by saving when you can so that the slower, leaner periods you will inevitably face will not have to feel or be so financially tight.

I am not a financial advisor, financial planner or CPA, but I do not think you have to be one to recognize that saving for a "rainy" day can never hurt.

I had a client who was lucky enough to land a series regular role in a network comedy that ran for five seasons. At a salary of about $20,000 per episode, with 24 episodes produced each year, it added up to a pretty respectable income, one that would, by almost any way you look at it, have given her more than enough money to live on with enough left over to invest or put away for later when the current job ended and before the next paying gig came along. If only.

Instead, this client could hardly keep her hands on her money. She spent it about as fast as it came it. Frequent, lavish, last-minute, first-class, weekend trips to five-star Hawaiian resorts can eat into one's profit margin very quickly. Even a financially successful, working actor with a business-savvy manager who kept telling her otherwise remained more intent on living for the moment than in securing for her financial future.

Not surprisingly, she eventually learned a high-priced lesson in fiscal stupidity.

Smart actors can, indeed, have satisfying careers that actually, even more-than-occasionally, earn them money for their acting work. Be smart about your money when that happens to you. But, in the meantime and in between those paying jobs, be just as smart about how you pay your own way day in and day out.

Fiscal Fitness

Part 2: Career Expenses

The good news is that as an independent businessperson, much of your business life becomes tax deductible, which can be of great benefit to you not just when you are actually earning big bucks as an actor, but all along your journey as you implement and stay on your action plan.

With the approach of any tax season, before you get too deep into what you might owe for the privilege of having worked in the business of acting, it is fiscally smart to take a good look at what it cost you, not just to generate the work, but what you spent, or rather invested, in *support* of your career.

It is important to set up a system that will help you easily keep track of the expenses you incur during the year so that you are prepared to take advantage of all of the write-offs and deductions you are legally entitled to take. It is true that you have to have earned money as an actor during the reporting year (and actually report it as income) in order to write off related expenses. But it is also true that the expenses you incur in the pursuit, development, education, training and growth of your career can be worth some money back into your pocket if you do it right and if you follow the legal rules.

Because you are your own business, you are entitled to file an IRS Schedule C with your 1040 tax return form. This is where you get to list all of the items you spent money on in support of your business during the year. Most actors know that the cost of photo sessions and photo reproductions are deductible. But you would be surprised to know that there is a large number of actors who either do not know or do not remember to deduct the costs of other key expenses, like the cost of your memberships to website services such as Actors Access and Casting Networks and the costs of those holiday cards you send or e-mail to your industry contacts (including postage).

Another often-overlooked deduction is the cost of parking when you go to an audition. Cash-strapped actors (even actors with lots of available cash) rarely will park in the rip-off garages or open lots at office buildings where the privilege of parking for the duration of an audition could easily set you back the cost of a week's worth of Starbucks lattes.

Street parking is usually the way to go, when you can find it (which is why it is always a good idea to plan to arrive at your audition location at least thirty minutes early so you will have plenty of time to hunt down a place to park without stressing that you might be late).

If you are a New York-based actor, the cost of bus fare, your MTA MetroCard or the occasional luxury of a cab ride can, as you know, add up pretty quickly. Get receipts, keep receipts and then remember you have these receipts for deductible expenses when it comes time to prepare your annual tax return.

The government wants to see receipts, but what can you do if you are dropping quarters and other loose change into parking meters that do not issue you a receipt? Many cities are swapping out old parking meters that take coins with new, electronic meters that take credit and debit cards. While the meter itself will not issue you a receipt for the transaction, you will see the charge on your credit card statement. Along with this "official" documentation of the expense, you will still need additional backup information to support the write-off.

Always keep a pad of small notepaper in your car with either a pen that works or with a pencil that actually has a sharpened point on the end of it. When you cannot get a receipt for what it cost you to park, write down all of the pertinent information on a piece of paper: day, date, time, location, how much money you put in the meter (or what the credit or debit charge is), the meter number and what the audition you went on was for. When you get home, put the piece of paper into the file folder labeled "Parking Expenses" that you have created just for this purpose. When that charge appears on your credit card or bank statement, make a copy of the statement, highlight the transaction and staple it to the note you made about the charge for backup reference, should you need it.

At the beginning of the next year, when you begin to add up what you have spent in support of your career, total up all of the receipts that you have generated and accumulated in the various categories you have incurred them in and *viola*! Now you have legitimate deductions.

Do the same thing for whatever expenses you incur going on or getting to an audition or acting job. New York-based actors are more likely to need a file labeled "Transportation Expenses" rather than "Parking Expenses." Create the files you need to accommodate the legitimate, deductible (and/or potentially deductible) expenses you incur. We will get into more detail on setting up a business expense filing system in a moment.

Of course, parking and transportation expenses incurred during the course of conducting your business during the year are not just limited to when you go to an audition. Parking for or transportation to/from a class, parking for or transportation to/from a meeting with your agent or manager, parking at or transportation to/from the cineplex or independent movie theatre to screen the new George Clooney film to study his process of character development—it is all money spent in the development of your career.

If you own an automobile (that lets out most New Yorker City actors), even the mileage you drive to and from these career-related activities can be written off as a percentage against your earned income.

I am not a CPA, but I am, like you, a business of acting business person. I have learned a lot over the years from my own CPA and financial guru, Christopher Debbini. At least I can pass some of that on to you. As businesspeople, we are entitled to write-offs that employees are not. The worse thing that you could do is to not take advantage of what might be due you in return for filing your return.

The best way that I have found to maximize these deductions you may be entitled to take is to set up a filing system that will help you manage these potential year-end write offs throughout the year. Your practice of shoving receipts into an old shoebox (if you kept them at all) is over. Priority one: keep receipts for everything and file them, as you incur them, into the appropriate file, detailing on each receipt what the expense was for. Remember, if it is transportation to an audition or parking for a business meeting, write down what the audition was for or who the meeting was with.

Every receipt should have a date on it and as much applicable information about the expense incurred as you think might be necessary to defend the deduction, should you ever have to do so.

Start this project by making a list of the categories that your legitimate business expenses fall into. In addition to the ones mentioned above, your list should also include subscription expenses for self-submission casting services like Actors Access and Casting Networks; website expenses for the design, maintenance and hosting of your business website; ISP fees for your online access; professional services for legal, business and career advising; coaching, classes, seminars and workshops for your business development; commissions you pay your agent and/or manager; business entertainment expenses for when you take your agent or manager to lunch to discuss your action plan and career strategy; cell phone, PDA, text-messaging expenses to the extent the device and services are used for your business; head shots and hard copy head shot reproductions; demo reel production; the costs to upload and maintain your support materials (head shots and demo reels) on a professional online site; publicity, PR, marketing and promotion costs for your business, your brand and your career; and professional dues to a union and/or legitimate, professional theatre company you may belong to.

If you drive to an audition or other business-related appointment, keep track of the mileage driven to and from your destination. Every business mile driven has a potential tax-deductible value. At the end of the year, when you calculate how many miles you drove for business that year against how many miles you drove in total that year, you will be able to determine what percentage of your vehicle was used for business and what percentage was used personally. This calculation will then determine what percentage of the automobile expenses you incurred that year (gas, oil, maintenance, repair, insurance) can be deducted as a business expense.

There are more categories and calculations, but you do not have to have been a math major to do this. You will find a worksheet template at the end of this chapter that will jumpstart you on your way to preparing and customizing your own personal list of business expense categories.

The services of a professional tax preparer or CPA (also deductible) who is familiar with the business of acting should be sought out to advise you further. It is not that your local H&R Block or family tax person could not do this for you; it is just that we in the business of acting are entitled to categories of deductions that, while considered legitimate for us, would be a red flag for an audit for a non-business of acting business.

A tax professional who is experienced in dealing with people like us and businesses like ours can help in maximizing what you are legally entitled to deduct.

For example, while you can deduct the cost of movie or theatre tickets to study a project or review a performance for your own career enhancement (or to benefit you in an upcoming audition or project of your own), your cousin who works in a medical office or your best friend who is a bank loan officer would not be allowed such deductions under normal circumstances.

When should you seek the advice of a professional tax planner? As soon as possible. You may not make enough money from your craft in the early years of your career to become a regular client yet, but, if in year five, you suddenly hit the financial jackpot, you stand to attract the attention of the IRS who will want to know why and what preceded this financial win.

For that reason alone, you want to keep accurate records from the beginning and be smart about how you plan for your financial future and your tax liability that comes with achieving the career success you seek.

Do not throw any of your business receipts away for at least seven years. Should you ever become targeted for an IRS tax audit, your returns for several of the previous years can be examined, so you want to be prepared and ready to defend your categories and calculations if called upon to do so. My personal and business tax advisor and every other professional I have talked with about this suggests that nothing less than seven years of tax files and receipts should be saved.

Deductions are always weighed against income. You cannot get refunded money you have not paid in, which brings up one more important part of this discussion.

As an actor, you will be hired, generally, in one of four categories: 1) to be paid as an independent contractor, 2) to be paid as an employee, 3) to work for deferred payment or 4) to work for free.

Being paid as an independent contractor means that you will be paid the amount agreed upon and accepted by you and then issued payment for that amount in full. No taxes will be deducted from your check, which means two things: 1) at the end of the year, you will be sent a 1099 form from the employer that indicates your earnings and 2) you are responsible for paying taxes due on those earnings.

Usually a 1099 person is required to pay estimated taxes quarterly in an amount that estimates what should be close to your full tax liability for the year.

The upside of establishing independent contractor status is that the Schedule C you will file to claim your business write-offs as a part of your annual tax return is an expected component of that return. If you are declared to have employee status, the issue of claiming "non-reimbursed employee expenses," rather than Schedule C expenses as an independent contractor, might come into play. More about employee status shortly.

There are detailed, legal rules and regulations that both employer and independent contractor must follow and strictly adhere to for both of you to claim and maintain your independent contractor status. But, if you follow the requirements, it can prove to be a valuable classification for both of you.

Not being an attorney, I also want to advise you to do some research on what it means to be an independent contractor from the IRS's perspective. You can find this information by looking on the IRS website at irs.gov. There is also a Self-Employed Individuals Tax Center accessible through that site where you will find a lot of helpful information on this and other related topics.

If you are hired and paid for an acting job as an employee (which is more likely the case when you get hired for a long-term or ongoing project like a film, a television series or Equity stage production), taxes will automatically be deducted from each paycheck you receive. While, in many cases, an independent contractor is trying to decrease the amount of taxes they will have to pay into the system upfront, an employee is trying to maximize the legitimate refund they are entitled to receive from taxes already paid in.

Either way, any claim of any business-related or business-incurred expenses must be justifiable and have actually been expended in the course of conducting or engaging in your business or business-related activities.

Deferred-payment work situations are likely on small, often SAG-sanctioned short films (read: low budget) projects and/or films for festival submission, whereby you agree to work on the project for payment later, should the film owners receive compensation for the resulting product.

I have been representing actors for a long time and many have participated in projects label "deferred payment" and, to date, none (that I can recall) has ever received a deferred payment for their work. This is not to say that you should not get involved with a project classified in this category. It is more to say that if you decide to do so, do it for all of the right reasons—maybe it is a role you would really like to play, perhaps it is a script you really love, possibly it is a director you would really love to work with, etc.—but do not get involved for the well-intentioned promise of pay-for-play later.

Having said that, any business-related expenses you incur because of your participation in a project like this are all potentially deductible, as they would be for an actor with an independent contractor or employee classification.

Acting for free speaks for itself. Often, in the early launch of a career, working without financial compensation is the only way you can begin to build your professional acting resume—and I encourage you to do so. While you may not earn a paycheck, you will earn the experience every actor needs, particularly early on in your career journey, to propel you forward—and the truth is that even as your career builds you might come upon a role you really want to play or a project you otherwise want to get involved with that will not offer you money, but can offer you opportunity. The smart actor always recognizes and can distinguish the difference between "cost" and "value."

I meet actors all the time who tell me, after hearing me talk about fiscal responsibility, that all they want to do is act. I get it. But that attitude is short-sighted and will not serve those people well in the long run, if there is a long run of their careers at all. I am not suggesting that you become a part-time, amateur accountant. What I am asking is that you develop a fiscal awareness of what it takes, financially, to live and lead a normal life and what it will require, financially, to launch your action plan and support your career.

Two of the big reasons actors give up on both their dreams and their career pursuits is lack of perceived opportunity and shortness of funds. Young actors, in particular, who are making the transition from academia (where, usually, their housing and food were not costs they directly incurred) to the real world (where parents are all too eager or otherwise need to cut back on the financial support of their child) can quickly come face-to-face with the harsh realities of accepting the financial responsibilities of being a career-pursuing adult.

Do not let this be you.

Create and implement an action plan that includes both career and financial strategies in which you also accept the career and financial responsibilities that come with this commitment. Eventually, if it all goes according to plan, you will be so successful that you will need the services of a business manager (also deductible!) to handle the complicated finances of your growing business and your career.

Until that time, taking care of all of the aspects of your business must be your personal responsibility from day one.

BUSINESS EXPENSE WORKSHEET

I have created a starter template for you to refer to as you begin to create a financial filing system to organize and keep track of your career-related expenses.

Begin by getting a box of file folders. Label one each to the specific categories you expect to incur expenses in. Next file these folders into a file cabinet or bankers box for easy assess.

Early in each new year, as the tax forms due you begin to arrive, start adding up your expenses in each category and then enter these amounts on a worksheet like the one below. These categories and figures will become your Schedule C deductions with the annual tax return you file.

You may discover the need for additional categories as your action plan spreads throughout the year. Add new files as needed. At the end of the year, on each December 31 at midnight, consider your records for that year closed and create a fresh set of files for your new year business activity expenses.

Business Expense Worksheet
Tax year: _____

Auto expenses:	$_____
Auto insurance:	$_____
Auto repair:	$_____
Books, publications, subscriptions:	$_____
Business promotion and entertainment:	$_____
Cable (or satellite) television service:	$_____
Coaching, classes, seminars:	$_____
Commissions paid:	$_____
Demo reels:	$_____
Hair care and make-up supplies:	$_____
Internet Service Provider:	$_____
Mailing supplies:	$_____
Parking:	$_____
Photos:	$_____
Postage/delivery services:	$_____
Professional dues:	$_____
Professional fees:	$_____
Professional services:	$_____
Publicity, PR, marketing:	$_____
Review of plays, films, DVDs:	$_____
Software:	$_____
Telephone:	$_____
Transportation expenses:	$_____
Travel:	$_____
Website expenses:	$_____

CHAPTER 10

IT's ALL ABOUT THE PLAN:

Create and Launch Your Action Plan
for Career Success

WHY DO YOU need an action plan? For the same reason that a ship's rudder cannot keep the vessel on course without a captain to steer it, everything that moves needs a driver who possesses both a plan and a map to guide it and the ability to easily alter the course as or if necessary.

No business that has "ongoing success" as the results of the launch and growth of the entity can stand a solid chance of achieving that goal without a solid, smart and strategic plan to get there. Your action plan for career success can only be created when you feel ready for the assignment.

You cannot do this overnight or on a weekend. An action plan, like the career it will guide, is a work in progress—and the plan cannot be conceived, nor can it be implemented, until you feel ready for both the commitment and the challenge of the creation of the plan and the soon-to-follow launch of the journey it will take you on.

Your action plan will keep you focused on achieving the results you seek and help you manage the distractions that will inevitably occur along the way. Even the most perfect-appearing and well-thought-out plan can be interrupted or sidelined by the unexpected and unplanned-for circumstances that life throws our way.

While none of us can do much about that, having a solid action plan in place will allow you easy access to the on-ramp that will take you back to the place you left off and get you back up to speed again quickly.

This is not a race. It is not the finish line you should be focusing on, but, instead, the implementation of the tasks you have outlined for yourself in your proactive work to achieve your long-term goals.

The creation of an action plan that will serve you from day one must be rooted in developing an action plan that is not a chore to follow. It's kind of like a diet. It will not work unless you stick to it. It is likely that you will have the occasional day or few days where you find it impossible to stick to and stay on—and that is okay. There is no long-term damage done, as long as you find the passion to get back on it and focus on where it will take you, not where you have not been or have been unable to get to yet.

You cannot launch a plan without first learning the skills you will need to create the strategy required to build the action plan you need to lead you to the career you want. Having traveled through the journey of this book, you should now be ready to tackle this assignment with a clear head and a keen eye on generating results.

So, now, let's get down to business.

Whereas in the talent casting process, it is not the best actor, but the right actor, who gets the job, the same understanding needs to be applied to the process of creating and launching your action plan, whether at the beginning or for the reinvention of your career.

It is all rooted in the information that you gather about the business in which you intend to thrive, how that information you gather applies directly to you, and how you use it.

The level of competition to gain visibility, to create awareness and to assemble the professional partnerships you will need for the long haul of your journey will seem, at times, daunting.

Among the biggest mistakes young actors, in particular, make is in expecting results too soon. You cannot rush this process—and what works for one person, will not (necessarily) work for you. I am a big believer in customized action plans, not templates. A template will work for the format, but for the implementation and the specifics, your action plan has to be a written document that you can embrace bit by bit, that will encourage and embrace your passion for the process.

It is all about establishing work-in-progress goals and then doing the proactive work that will be required to achieve them. Managing expectations, a critical responsibility that has been addressed several times in this book, is essential.

Setting your sights on lofty goals that no action plan alone could achieve will only set you up for the frustration, the disappointment and the emotional unfitness that comes from hitting brick walls, arriving at dead ends and never feeling the joy of achieving a successful moment. Do not be that person. Instead, be and remain a smart actor by incorporating meaningful tasks that are routinely achievable by you on a regular basis.

Idealism, in place of realism, will result in failure.

Key to creating a successful action plan are some of the rules of the launch, before takeoff.

They are:

- ✦ Never take rejection personally, unless you were rejected because of something inappropriate or unprofessional that you did (it is your product or brand they may have chosen to pass on, not *you* personally).
- ✦ Your acting talent is a service that you provide to the entertainment community.
- ✦ The forward movement of your career requires that your action plan be a work in progress. While at the launch, your plan is in place. But your plan must be adaptable to circumstances, environment, and personal and professional conditions that may indicate that a change in plans is both in order and in the best interest of achieving the results you seek.

The acting business is an industry where success has little, if anything at all, to do with talent, training, education or credentials, but you cannot have any semblance of a career or the real, long-term success you seek without this foundation. While these things are, indeed, the hallmarks on which to build a career, success in this business, instead, has *everything* to do with opportunity, timing and an actor's readiness to assume and to deliver, on time, the tasks assigned. Opportunity opens doors; preparedness makes you ready to take full advantage of those situations when they come your way.

A successful action plan requires a commitment to a balanced endeavor that focuses on goals and tasks: Goals to achieve and tasks to implement to attain those goals.

Your action plan should include a day-by-day, week-by-week breakdown of what you intend to accomplish during a given period of time. It's not all work. Even the action plan of an uber-dedicated person should have contained in it time off for visits with family and friends, trips to the gym, going to the movies, whatever it takes to clear your head and give you some downtime away from your job of full-time plan implementation.

If you are not a new arrival to the business of acting, I assume that you have probably undertaken many independent tasks previously to get your career moving. It is important to forget about those past attempts right now. Whether you have or have not done so, whether those efforts were or were not successful does not matter. From this point on, we are starting with a clean slate on which to work.

An action plan works best when it is created from the last page working backwards. This approach keeps you focused on what you strive to achieve and allows you to construct what you need to do to get there. It is also a way to keep your plan pliable as the initial structure comes together.

While I cannot create your action plan for you, I am going to suggest a series of tasks that should be an ongoing part of your launch, implementation and maintenance activities. Whatever you use to track your appointments and other important dates, start a brand new calendar, digital template, iPhone or iPad calendar. Whatever you rely on to remind you of what comes next on the agenda of your life, create a new field or space in which to plan out the business of your career and learn to follow through on every entry.

The goal is building a career. Every action plan should include these tasks toward achieving that result:

✦ Self-Submission Services:

Create personal accounts at each of the professional casting submission services available for actors' use, which, as of this writing, include Actors Access, Casting Networks and The Casting Frontier. You may learn about others that you deem, after careful research, are valid, legitimate and worthy of your investment of time and dollars. Before committing to any service for which you will incur a fee, you should always perform due diligence in ascertaining the value, the follow-through and the effectiveness of the service before giving over any financial information that will be used to bill you.

It goes without saying, but it is worthy of saying nonetheless: never, ever, give your social security number to any such service. While you will be asked to complete rather extensive personal profiles on the sites mentioned (and others that you have checked out and decided to align with), this is information that is accessed potentially by both you and your representative(s) in making submissions for auditions.

You will never be asked by any legitimate service provider to enter anything as crucial to your identity protection as your social security number. I stress this to you now to help you avoid the occasions where (not you, but) overzealous, mostly young, actors, in the process of setting up self-submission casting accounts on services they had not checked out first, became so involved in the process that they willingly gave up more personal information than they needed to (or should have) and ended up creating situations to manage that were painfully difficult to undo or fix.

If you have already established accounts at any of these services listed above or any other that you have proven to yourself to be legitimate, then one of your action plan tasks must be to review and update your profile information at least once a month. If it has been too long since you have added new photos (especially if you have started to look in any way different from the photos previously uploaded to the site), replace them with new ones as soon as possible, if not immediately. More about this in a moment.

If you are creating new accounts, you must have at least one great, killer photo to upload as the cornerstone of your profile. Never create a profile without having a photo to go with it.

Self-submission services will only work for you if you are smart, strategic and as thoughtful as possible in both how you use them and what you expect out of them. Key to the effectiveness of using any of these services is not only how you use them, but also how often and when you use them.

Part of your action plan must be the commitment to get online at least three times a day (morning, afternoon and evening), making the time needed to read and carefully review all casting opportunities to carefully determine if you should submit on the listings or not.

New entries on the major services (Actors Access, Casting Networks, etc.) are released throughout the day and often evening, so it is imperative to that you stick to your action plan schedule to routinely check these potential opportunities, even on weekends.

Most casting directors who make breakdowns available for actors to submit directly expect that, if you determine that you are right for a role, you will submit on it immediately—and you cannot submit "immediately" unless you are on these sites searching, evaluating and taking action (or not) on a routine and regular basis.

I have met many actors who admit to checking self-submit

opportunities every few days. By then, it is too late. If self-submitting is a focal point of your action plan, and it should be, then make the time to take the action to do so on a schedule that will maximize the potential of both your efforts and your financial investment in your subscriptions to these online services.

✦ *Head Shots:*

Head shots are priority one. If you have photos that you like that have been working for you and are not outdated, then continue to use them, for now. However, my preference is that with the creation and launch of a (new) action plan, your tools should also be fresh and new. As we discussed in the chapter on "The Art of the Head Shot," there is no more critical tool that you will need than at least one head shot that reflects accurately and honestly the person you are now and the work-in-progress actor you are becoming.

Your action plan must include your honest monitoring of how you appear in body, what you look like facially and whether the head shot or head shots you are using are representative of your total image and your brand and are always one hundred percent accurate. Always.

✦ *Resume Review:*

Always keep your resume current and honest. The chapter on how to create an effective online and hard-copy resume gave you suggestions on what to put in and what to leave out, all in an attempt to help define what kind of actor you are right now and what kind of actor you have the potential to become.

Any time you have a new item to add to any section of your resume, do it right away. Your action plan should include your weekly review of the resume you have created online for the various casting submission services. While you may not have something new to add each week (and odds are, you will not), keeping tabs on this document is important to do.

Entries that prove the results of your proactive action plan, such as new skills acquired and new classes taken, can be more beneficial for a particularly young, new-to-the-business actor than even a new acting credit (of course, depending on what that credit is).

Any change you make to your online resume needs to be made to your hard copy resume, as well, so that the information that appears on the back of the hard copy head shot you take with you to your auditions always reflects *exactly* the same information the casting director looked at online to determine to call you in.

✦ *Classes, Workshops and Seminars:*

An actor acts. When you are not acting (or working to earn the funds required to support both your action plan and your career), you must be in a class. Your action plan needs to include time to research training opportunities, including time to audit a session of a new class you are thinking of signing up for.

Classes come in all shapes and sizes and can range from one afternoon to multi-week and ongoing programs.

There are a lot of ineffective classes taught by underqualified acting teachers, but there are also many terrific opportunities for training with some very gifted, passionate teachers. Search out these great opportunities with your smart actor filter in place as you evaluate and assess various programs and teachers.

What classes are your actor friends taking? Which teachers have you heard about? Online and (still, as of this writing) print publications each have their share of ads for coaches, classes and workshops. If you haven't got a clue where to begin, start your research there.

Your action plan should require you to be in a class at least once a week (and more often, if you can afford it).

✦ *Self-Support:*

You cannot achieve much with any action plan unless or until you can fund it. Without the tools in place that you will need to dig through the work to be done, it will be a slow, frustrating and, usually, ineffective and unsuccessful effort.

Get a job. Fiscal fitness is your personal responsibility for first funding your life and then supporting your career journey. As we discussed in the chapter on "Emotional, Physical and Fiscal Fitness in the New Landscape," it may not be the support job of your dreams, but until your acting career can pay your bills (or at least some of them), you must create an opportunity to meet the financial obligations life requires of all of us.

Using the concept of The Business of Acting Gift Registry® introduced earlier in the book can be an effective way of letting those who love you help support your professional life by helping you pay for those related expenses.

Another one of the biggest mistakes actors make is in not realistically calculating and then accumulating the amount of money they will need to fund their action plans. If the dollars do not yet exist to launch the plan and implement the strategy, then delay the process until it can be done right.

✦ *Personal Exposure:*

Seek out opportunities not just to grow your career, but to build your community. Do not let your professional pursuits isolate you. Indeed, this is a very social business, but if your opportunities to mingle with other actors exist only at auditions and in classes, you will limit your ability to see, to be seen and to network.

Recently I was a panelist at a major show business expo at the Los Angeles Convention Center. I couldn't help but notice what appeared to be hundreds of people mingling about in dark shirts and red ties eager to answer questions and to direct expo guests and visitors to the various activities at the event. I later learned that all of these people (most of them actors) had volunteered their time for the weekend for the opportunity to be a part of the event and have the chance to meet and chat with a lot of people who are already connected in the industry they seek to succeed in. Smart actors.

Your action plan should include a specific day, date and time at least once a week for you to research local industry-related events, ranging from film festivals to conventions and conferences, where you can volunteer some time to get involved, give back and take away some potentially important information—and make some potentially important connections. Check into volunteer opportunities at the Academy of Motion Picture Arts & Sciences, the Academy of Television Arts & Sciences and other respected industry organizations and groups.

Check for free events to attend, including industry author book signings at retail stores and libraries and industry-related activities that are offered up for members of groups you might already belong to, such as networking events served up by Actors Access and Casting Networks.

Once you have earned union membership, I urge you to learn everything you can about the work of SAG Foundation and the ongoing events and networking sessions they offer to union members for free. I have been very impressed with the quality and range of professional, career-related activities available to union members through this organization.

✦ Create a "Hit" List:

Your action plan should include the creation of a work-in-progress professional "hit" list of industry professionals you want to target your outreach to. Start with the people who cast the television shows you would like to audition for. Include the casting directors for local and nearby regional theatre companies. Include agents and managers who represent actors like you. Do *not* include the large, major agents, managers and/or agencies unless your resume supports the entry and the subsequent contact.

Create a hit list that is appropriate for who you are right now, where you are right now and the strategy behind the action plan you have designed.

This is not about creating a list heavy with impressive names, but light on reality. It needs to be a list of people that it makes sense for you to reach out to, both for you and for those on the list. A starter list of ten great, smartly targeted contacts is far better and potentially more effective and beneficial to you than a list of 50 people who make no sense to include.

There are many sources of credible contact information. The trade hard copy and online publication *Daily Variety* offers access to television and film production charts on their website at variety.com that lists the names and contact information for most key players involved with most in-development and current projects.

Also, IMDb.com is a terrific and generally accurate source of names, numbers and other contact information for industry professionals. It requires (as of this writing) a subscription to their IMDbPro service to access this information, but if you can work this minimal cost into your action plan budget, it will be well worth it for two reasons: first, the availability to research anyone in the business of acting (from actor to producer to casting director) and most projects (from television series to feature films to direct-to-video productions) can save you hours of random online research time and provide trusted information from an industry-used and industry-respected resource; secondly, becoming a subscriber will allow you to upload your own head shot and resume to the site, which then creates a profile for you and on you that anyone in the industry (and others) can access.

As you begin to work and to accumulate the television and film credits (and/or Broadway credits which are archived on the service's companion site IBDB.com, the Internet Broadway Database) that meet the qualifications to be listed on the site, you can submit them to be added to your profile (although most production companies will routinely submit information on their projects, including casting, directly to the site, which will resulting in a credit listing automatically appearing on your site profile page).

As you work, as you study, as you move through your action plan and as you meet new industry professionals, add them to your hit list. Your hit list should also be used to target the industry professionals whom you would like to meet.

I am a big advocate of the informational interview. While a targeted agent or manager may not be signing clients (or seeking clients in your category) at the time of your inquiry, you may find that, surprisingly perhaps, many will be willing to sit with you for a short meeting during which time you can ask questions, gain advice and add to your networking achievements.

The same holds true with casting directors. While many casting directors meet new-to-the-business actors at workshops these actors pay to attend, many still meet new actors the old-fashioned way, through general meetings.

Your action plan should include contacting at least one agent, manager or casting director you have not yet met every week in an attempt to secure at least one informational meeting each month.

I also encourage you to also create a personal hit list. When something noteworthy or newsworthy happens for you in business, let the community you call your own (family, friends, teachers, etc.) also know about it.

✦ *Professional Marketing:*

Proactive outreach is a critical part of your action plan, but so, too, must be the information you plant for others to find or to stumble upon.

While the practice of sending out hard copy postcards to agents, managers and casting directors has declined enormously in the new business of acting, there are still many in professionals in the business who still like getting (and encourage actors to send) these kinds of notices. If you have something to announce (you have just landed a role in a project that is worthy of seeking attention for, you have just booked a standout role in a national commercial, you have just been cast in a nice role in a local stage production), then create a marketing mailing to promote the achievement.

Typically, a hard copy version of this kind of brand PR piece will have your photo on the front side and the related text with your announcement information on half of the back side, along with, of course, your name and your contact information.

Always leave sufficient space to place an address label and a postage stamp on the back of your hard copy postcard—and check and double check that it all looks right before you print it, whether you do this on your home computer or have an outside service print it for you.

I remind you of this because not checking the details can be costly in many ways.

During the final, hectic weeks before one of our end-of-semester Business of Acting class showcases, the students, whose final project was both producing and performing in the industry-invited event, forgot to (or did not know to) check both their postcard measurements and a proof before printing it. As a result, their postcards came back from the printer with the brand image on the front looking as intended, but the related text on the back taking up the entire back side of the card, leaving no room for a mailing label or a stamp.

If you do not take the time to get it right the first time, the costs of fixing it (meaning a rush reprinting job) will easily and quickly put you over budget.

In the new business of acting, many casting directors are also accepting digital postcards by e-mail, which offers up great savings all around, but still requires the attention to the details that are unique to electronic mailings, including file format, printability, font size readability that works on a variety of screens and devices, etc.

At the top of the best way to continually market your brand, through your proactive action plan and to those who will seek you out, is through a dedicated business website for you and your career. There is nothing personal about this. If you want to have a website to showcase family and friend photos or to write a blog, that's great. But do not do that on, or make it a part of, your business website.

Your professional website should, if available and if possible, be your name at a .com address. If you already use your name domain for a personal site, get a new domain name for that purpose and use the other exclusively for business. Part of your brand is your name—and name awareness and name recognition is a crucial component in building a career and a brand.

Use a website creation service—or if you are one of those tech-savvy, brilliant people who can do this on your own, even better, then create your business website on your own. But remember, site visitors will judge you and your brand by how both are packaged and presented. Looks count here. If your business website does not look like it deserves to be viewed, then it will not, relegating it to "just another actor's website" status.

Do not let this be the perception of you, your career and your brand. Do this the right way from the beginning. There are numerous professional website building options and services available to you; some are already in the business of creating, designing and hosting sites for actors and can be found online or through the professional casting services.

Whether you already have a lot of material to work with or all you have is a head shot, resume and bio to begin with, grow your website as you build your career.

Your website does not have to have all the bells and whistles right from the start—or maybe ever. It is about what is appropriate for you. It needs to be a great presentation of your brand and can eventually grow to include individual video clips from work that you do, a demo reel that collects some of your best work and showcases it in a short video, production stills taken on the set while you are working, reviews and, of course, a constantly updated bio and resume.

Your website must also contain contact information for you and for the people who represent you (if you are represented or when you become represented).

Lastly, through services such as Google AdSense and others, you can arrange for ads to appear on your website for which you will be compensated based on a variety of factors, including the number of click-throughs an ad receives from your site. While this may generate some minor income for you, do *not* do this on your professional business site. Ads on your site will serve as distractions, not enhancements. Your business website is about you and your brand, not about anything else anybody else is selling.

A final word about the public career announcements you make about yourself, whether on your website, in a blog or in a hard copy mailing: *never* announce a casting assignment unless you have cleared the way to do so. The ability for the quick release of casting and other production information by actors, that has been considered confidential until officially announced by the company producing the project, has caught many studios, producers and publicists by surprise—and it is never a happy surprise.

Most casting and production information is considered confidential for very specific reasons. Even in your excitement over getting cast in the role of a lifetime that will make your career, do not *ever* discuss or otherwise release publicly any information that you have not first asked permission to reveal. It could cost you the job.

✦ *Monitor Your Brand:*

It has never been easier to track what is being said or written about you and your brand. In the old days, we had to subscribe to expensive news clipping services that would have dozens of employees whose jobs it was to quickly and accurately read just about every major print publication you could name, both locally and nationally, hunting and scanning for the mention of subscribers' names (both individuals and companies). Whenever a hit was found, the article was literally clipped out of the publication, put into an envelope and mailed to the subscriber once or twice a week.

It was a very slow process and it often took weeks or even a month or more to get a clipping of a "current" item. By then, of course, while it was nice to know what coverage you or your company got, it was clearly old news. Should a clipping turn up that had information within it that was inaccurate or otherwise needed action of some sort, it was often too late to be very effective in seeking a retraction, a correction or fixing a problem.

That was then. Today we all have the availability, the luxury really, to monitor almost anything that appears about us in print, online or even on broadcast/cable outlets – and we get to do it for free. I cannot underscore the tremendous value this affords all of us who have a brand to maintain, an image to protect and a public presence to monitor.

Through services such as Google New Alerts and Yahoo! Alerts, you can create notification systems that operate off of key words, such as your name. Whenever the 24/7 Internet scanning system detects the appearance of your entered key word or words, you will receive an alert by e-mail informing you that somewhere, someone or some entity has posted something that may be about you.

Take full advantage of these opportunities to monitor both your name and your brand. We do this for every client on our roster. We also do this for every project the client gets cast in. In a global marketplace where you never know what may be or is being said about you anywhere on the planet, this is a great way to keep on top of news that matters most to your business: news about you.

Every action plan should include setting up the online accounts needed to access these free services and then checking every alert you receive right away.

✦ *Budget Your Time and Your Money:*

Your action plan will require both your time and your money to implement, to follow and to build on.

Plan to engage in your regular business activities on a regular schedule, not at random times. It is like taking prescription medication. You are instructed by someone who knows better than you when to take it, how often to take it and for how long to take it.

I am prescribing for you a consistent schedule on which to engage in these action tasks. Once, three times a day, for self-submission service entry reviewing; once a week for contacting an industry professional you have not yet met to request an informational meeting; and at least once a month for an informational meeting request fulfilled (of course, if the person you target to meet with cannot or will not meet with you, it is not your fault; move on).

You will have both one-time and ongoing, recurring expenses connected with your action plan. Head shots, a one-time fee; printing multiple hard copies of one head shot to take with you to auditions, a one-time fee; subscriptions to the online self-submission casting services, payment due each month or once a year for twelve months; classes, payment either upfront for a single meet session or payment in advance (or as you go, if you can arrange it) for more long-term sessions.

As you do your research to assemble and create your action plan, you will discover, in the process, the specific costs of each task you plan to undertake or item you will need to purchase. Map it out financially. The goal, in the best case scenario, is to pay as you go for every service you require and not build up credit card debt that can quickly become suffocating and impossible for you to get out from under. Finance your action plan by creating a budget that you can work with, stick to and live on.

Lastly, get and keep receipts for every action plan expense you incur. As we discussed in the chapter on "Emotional, Physical and Fiscal Fitness in the New Landscape," these expenses can add up quickly and can prove to be valuable deductions at the end of each tax year against any business of acting income you earn.

Every action plan needs to be customized to fit both the comfort level and availability of the person who creates it. While most action plans may, on the surface, seem similar, the tactical differences are in how the tasks committed to on the plan are executed. You define the terms of your business of acting action plan. You set the perimeters and goal posts from which to judge your progress. A successful plan is one that keeps you moving forward. A successful plan is also one that allows you the room to make changes, as/if needed, as you go along.

An action plan is a lifetime commitment. The goal is not just to get you up and running with your career at the beginning, but to keep you proactive through all of the stages and phases of your journey. Remember, it is not a final, end result that you should be seeking, but rather a path to a continuous stream of opportunities for you to embrace, for you to make your own and for you to build your career on.

CHAPTER 11

NOTES FOR THE BEGINNING OF YOUR JOURNEY

WHEN *The Business of Acting* was first published in 2002, I offered up ten personal notes for actors to serve as focal points, or reminders, to come back to when the road got bumpy or the plan did not seem to gel. While, clearly, so much has changed in the business of acting since then, a few things have held steady, like the need to never let your passion for what you seek to achieve wane, even when the going gets rougher than you would like or have planned for. These ten notes, though written for the start of a journey during a different time, actually feel even more applicable today.

So, whether you are about to launch your first action plan or have gone back to the drawing board in a proactive effort to review and restart anew, I hope that you will first and frequently consider these notes as suggestions for how to stay focused and keep moving forward.

- ✦ I am a work in progress.
- ✦ My career is a work in progress.

- ✦ I will view and react to my experiences in terms of black and white and not the colors of emotional stress.
- ✦ I will stay clear about my mission.
- ✦ I will continue to gather new materials and upgrade the tools I need for use along my journey.
- ✦ I will continually seek to acquire and to develop the skills that I will need to build, sustain and grow my career.
- ✦ I will begin (or relaunch) and fuel my journey with energy, enthusiasm and healthy motivation.
- ✦ I will temper my journey with patience, fortitude and self-reliance.
- ✦ I will live by a code of ethics that will serve to frame my intent along with my actions.
- ✦ I will follow my heart, follow my action plan and try to learn something new about myself and this business every day, each step of the way.

CHAPTER 12

AN ACTOR'S CODE OF ETHICS

W E ALL LIVE by a set of morals, standards and ethics that define our lives and our relationships. It was true when my first book was published and, in these times in which we all live, it seems important to revisit.

The business has changed, but how you weigh the choices you will be asked to make—and what sacrifices you are willing to endure to see your plan through and your dream realized—says a lot about how you value the opportunities that you will earn, in terms of the bigger picture of the life you lead.

When opportunity knocks, how will you recognize it? When your value system is challenged, how much might you be willing to compromise and at what price? Is the career success you seek worth the investment and the patience it will require to get there?

Add to the personal credo that guides you these fourteen proclamations that will help you answer these questions and help maintain your vision, your concentration and your positive attitude along your career journey in the new business of acting.

I end every class semester I teach and each workshop I give by reading these aloud to those in attendance. They help keep me grounded, as well, through the challenges I face with my own clients and in life. I hope that you, too, will find these to be grounding principles to make your own in a business where a code of ethics often seems nonexistent or a code open to interpretation.

They are:

+ I will be respectful of my fellow actors and helpful to them.
+ I will be supportive of my fellow actors, not competitive against them.
+ I will celebrate the successes of my fellow actors with them and not be jealous or envious of what may, at first, seem to me to be their good fortune.
+ I recognize that no fellow actor has the ability to take away from me any opportunity that is meant to be mine. We will each get what is ours to get.
+ I will not sell out.
+ I recognize that I do not now know everything that I am going to need to know to have the professional career I desire.
+ I will never doubt my ability. But I also recognize that my ability, like my potential, will grow only if I nurture it in a healthy environment.
+ I will value my friends and my family more than any professional opportunity, for I can be driven and motivated without becoming distant and removed from those I care most about.
+ I will always be true to my passion and to myself by recognizing that every professional journey needs a happy, challenged and fulfilled navigator.

- I recognize that there is a difference between what I am given and what I earn.
- I will never lose my true sense of self in the perception that others may have of me.
- I will sometimes not talk, but rather just listen to what the world around me and those I cherish have to say. I recognize that sometimes they will know more than I do.
- I will give back to my community, my family and my friends in ways that say that I value what I have gotten from them.
- If any day on my journey ever seems to be too great a struggle or delivers too great an accolade, I will remember, simply, that tomorrow is another day.

CHAPTER 13

RESOURCES FOR ACTORS

THE RESOURCES PAGE on our website, at TheBusinessOfActing.com, is loaded with helpful resources for actors at all stages of their careers. From recommendations of head shot photographers and coaches to direct links to the actor unions, you will find everything you need to get started—or restarted—on your career journey on that page.

We also encourage you to view the collection of exclusive interview segments with successful, working actors and other industry professionals featured on our Web TV series *Inside the Business of Acting* for some no-nonsense advice on how to launch and build a career in this business. You will find a complete list of all of the available interviews and have access to view them at InsideThe BusinessOfActing.com.

We are constantly updating and revising the listings on the site. If you discover one that we should know about, please let us know at Inquiries@TheBusinessOfActing.com.

CHAPTER 14

WEBSITES REFERENCED IN
THE NEW BUSINESS OF ACTING

T HE NEW business of acting has generated an array of outstanding, professional online resources for actors. Unfortunately, there have also been many more sites created that should be avoided under any circumstances. You have an obligation to both the integrity of your brand and to your wallet to perform due diligence in checking out the legitimacy of any online (or other) service you are considering using as part of your action plan.

Here is a list of the sites referenced in this book:

alliance.org.au (Media Entertainment and Arts Alliance, Australia)

ActorsAccess.com

ActorsEquity.org

actra.com (Alliance of Canadian Cinema, Television and Radio Artists)

agma.org (American Guild of Musical Artists)

aftra.com (American Federation of Television and Radio Artists)

backstage.com

CastingNetworks.com

equity.org/uk (Equity/United Kingdom)

HollywoodReporter.com

IBDB.com (Internet Broadway Database)

IMDb.com (Internet Movie Database)

InsideTheBusinessOfActing.com

irs.gov (Internal Revenue Service)

LACasting.com (L.A. Casting)

LemackCo.com (Lemack & Company Talent Management/ Public Relations)

NYCasting.com (New York Casting)

sag.org (Screen Actors Guild)

SFCasting.com (San Francisco Casting)

TheBusinessOfActing.com

TheCastingFrontier.com

variety.com

CHAPTER 15

THE LAST WORD...

YOU CAN DO THIS.

You have the talent within you to go the long haul. You have the potential within you to go the distance—and now you have the skills you need to build the career you want in the landscape that is the new business of acting.

No book can deliver your dreams to you. That you have to work for and earn yourself. But what you have learned about yourself, about the process and about what is both expected and required of you to take this journey can open the doors to the opportunities you seek.

What kind of actor are you now? What kind of actor do you have the potential to become? What kind of actor do you want to be?

Stay focused, be confident and always work at being a smart businessperson in the process of growing your career, and anything is possible.

I wish you much luck, endless opportunity and all good fortune all along your journey.

NOTES

1. California Department of Industrial Relations—Talent Agency Case TAC No. 19-90 (4/24/92) (http://www.dir.ca.gov/dlse/dlse-tacs.htm)
2. Variety.com (9/21/03) (http://www.variety.com/article/VR1117892733.html)
3. Back Stage (9/01/06) (http://www.backstage.com/bso/esearch/article_display.jsp?vnu_content_id=1003086355)
4. Back Stage (9/01.06) (http://www.backstage.com/bso/esearch/article_display.jsp? vnu _content_id=1003086355)
5. tmz.com (7/27/09) (http://www.tmz.com/2009/07/27/ugly-lawsuit-filed-against-bettys-dad/)
6. California Department of Industrial Relations—Talent Agency Case TAC No. 63-93 (2/24/95) (http://www.dir.ca.gov/dlse/dlse-tacs.htm)
7. California Department of Industrial Relations—Talent Agency Case TAC No. 52-92 (6/02/94) (http://www.dir.ca.gov/dlse/dlse-tacs.htm)
8. California Department of Industrial Relations—Talent Agency Case TAC No. 21-00 (8/16/01) (http://www.dir.ca.gov/dlse/dlse-tacs.htm)
9. Hollywood Reporter (11/06/08)

Appendix:
About the Author

AFTER A TEN-YEAR on-air and production career in Boston radio and television, Brad Lemack relocated to Los Angeles in 1980 to accept a position as a publicity executive for pioneering TV producer Norman Lear's Tandem/TAT Productions (later Embassy Television). The numerous television series Brad was involved with included *Archie Bunker's Place*, *The Jeffersons*, *One Day at a Time*, *Square Pegs*, *Diff'rent Strokes* and *The Facts of Life*, as well as several movies for television, specials, syndicated series and pilots.

He left that position in 1982 to establish his own agency, Lemack & Company Talent Management/Public Relations (LemackCo. com).

Since then, Lemack & Company has established itself in the areas of talent management and career development for actors, and in entertainment, personality and non-profit public relations, and special event creation and production.

Brad manages a diverse list of established actors, performers and development clients. His cumulative career management and public relations client list includes Isabel Sanford, Sherman Hemsley, Marla Gibbs, Betsy Palmer, Beverly Garland, Regina King, Bonnie

Franklin, Alaina Reed, Kevin Peter Hall, Pamela Roylance, Henry Polic II, Basil Hoffman, Army Archerd, Eddie Albert, Elliott Gould, Liberace and Village People, to name a few (complete list at LemackCo.com).

As a Business of Acting Career Coach, he also leads workshops and seminars around the country, and consults with actors in smaller group meetings and individual sessions, on how to approach and manage the challenges and overcome the stumbling blocks they face in the pursuit of their careers.

Brad's first book, *The Business of Acting: Learn the Skills You Need to Build the Career You Want,* was first published in 2002, with subsequent reprinting.

He is the host of the Web TV series *Inside the Business of Acting* (InsideTheBusinessOfActing.com), which features conversations with successful, working actors and other industry professionals talking about their career journeys, turning points and lessons learned along the way, all designed to empower a global audience of young actors (and others) in the journeys of their own careers.

He also writes The Business of Acting Blog, at TheBusiness OfActing.com, where he offers commentary and perspective on current events in the business of acting and offers answers and solutions to readers' questions and to their industry challenges.

Brad has been a professor of performing arts and communication studies at the Emerson College Los Angeles Center since 1995. He teaches The Business of Acting, the course he created and developed for both students of the performing arts and students seeking careers in related fields within the industry. He also teaches a course in entertainment and interactive public relations.

In addition, in 2008 Brad launched the new media production company RerunIt, LLC, and serves as the company's President/ CEO. The company owns and operates the entertainment website

RerunIt.com, which features exclusive video packages and interview clips showcasing actors and media personalities who have helped shape and define American pop culture. Brad serves as the host for the collection of on-demand webcasts available on the site.

He received his Bachelor of Science degree in communications from Emerson College, in Boston, and his Master of Arts in theatre arts and dance, with a concentration in performance for social change, from California State University, Los Angeles.

Brad welcomes comments from readers of *The New Business of Acting* by either e-mail or postal mail. He can be reached at:

blemack@TheBusinessOfActing.com

or

Brad Lemack
c/o Ingenuity Press USA
P.O. Box 69822
Los Angeles, California 90069-0822